WHO KILLED
MARY GUNN?

SOLVING THE
PORTENCROSS MURDER MYSTERY

By

STEPHEN BROWN

Edited by Rebecca Catherine Brown

Published by
The Transparent Publishing Company

www.TransparentPublishing.co.uk

ISBN 9798670307246

The <u>cover photo</u> is a postcard from the author's collection. It was produced in the week following the murder and shows a postman wearing his rain cape, made to look as if he is a policeman guarding the scene of the crime. The postcard sold in the thousands throughout the area demonstrating the public interest in the case.

First published October 18th, 2018
Original Copyright holder – Stephen Brown

<u>Dedication</u>

To my Rebecca
(and her beautiful, beautiful hat!)

Preface

One of our favourite hobbies, my Dad and I, is watching crime shows on the television. Never did I expect that he would solve one himself. Thinking outside of the box, he has solved a riddle that has baffled many great minds before him: Who Killed Mary Gunn?

A narrative of jealousy, contempt and loathing, the tale of the Portencross Murder is one that will capture your attention from the outset. Through careful analyses of local newspapers and a reinterpretation of crime scene evidence that was perhaps previously overlooked, this chilling retelling of events proves just how powerful hindsight can be.

The evidence, as you will find, is compelling and tells a story of Edwardian scandal shrouded in secrecy. There are details overlooked that today's technology would surely prioritise. It is perhaps only with 21st century eyes that we are able to unpick the subtleties of the case and proceeding investigation.

I hope that my Dad knows just how proud we are of his hard work, ingenuity and constant innovation. I have never known a more rounded intelligence and can only hope one day to inspire others as he has inspired me.

- Rebecca Catherine Brown

WHO KILLED MARY GUNN?

CONTENTS

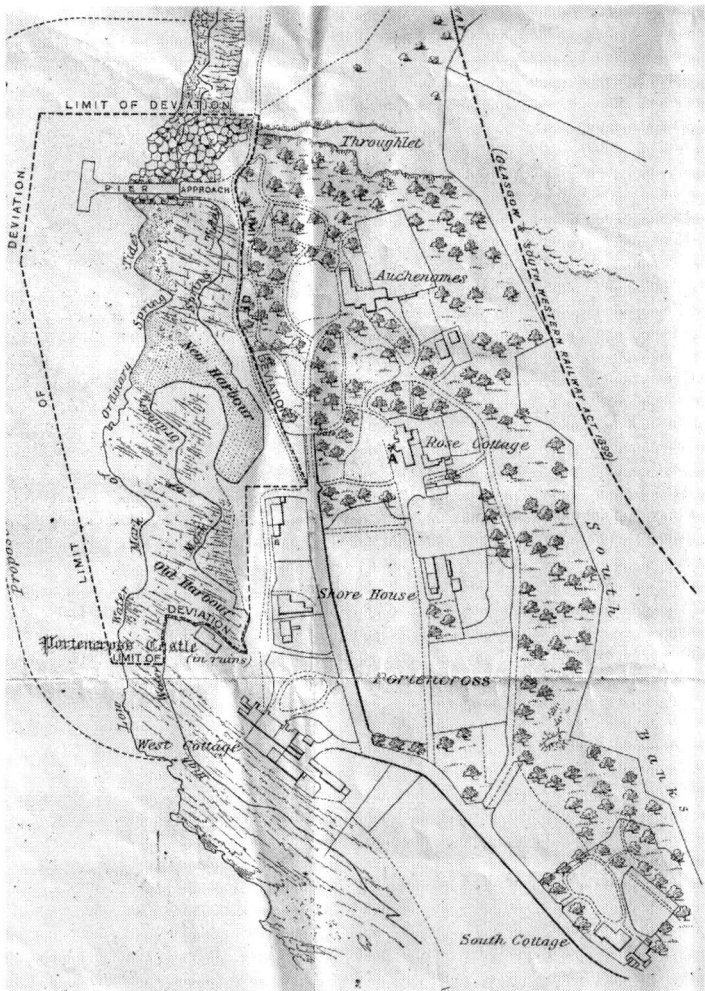

Above – a map of Portencross from 1911 showing the farm track leaving to the north (top). It was down this track that Alexander McLaren ran following the murder. He ran past the pier and entered the Auchenames estate by means of the gate and pathway shown. After he had phoned for the police he made his way to Law Farm, drawn to the right-hand side of the Shore Boarding House.

INTRODUCTION

There should be no doubt that Edwardian policing was in a mess as compared to how we view the efficiency of our modern-day force. Nowadays, we enjoy rattling good yarns by means of television, telling us how clever detective work, forensics or even crime scene investigation solved an intricate and sinister murder. Simply knowing of the vast resources that the state will deploy in the event of a murder crime might lead us to assume personal safety even in our own homes. Yet, here is a mystery that remains unsolved to this day despite the extensive efforts of many, many people.

Above – The murdered Mary Gunn

Mary Gunn, aged only 49, was shot a little over one hundred years ago. In the dead of a rainy night, as she and her family gathered around the fireside, a shot was fired through the window of the small and remote Scottish Cottage. The assailant was unknown.

Alexander McLaren was not originally from Ayrshire, but his wife Jessie and her younger sister Mary were brought up in Beith where their father had a business as a railway contractor. Alexander had met Jessie when he was the general store manager at the Ironworks in Dalry. In her youth, Mary Gunn had been regarded as a considerable beauty and mentioned as a possible contender in a beauty competition. There were three daughters in the family – Jessie being the oldest and Mary the youngest – the middle sister Eliza had immigrated to Canada some years before the Mary's murder.

Even to this day, the police seem none the wiser as to the identity of the murderer. Despite the case being "re-opened" several times since that dark day in 1913, it would appear that the investigation file and notes have been lost! After repeated requests, and red herring trails to Glasgow and Edinburgh, I have as yet had no sight of the illusory paperwork.

Therefore, the following can only be my

reasonable discourse on the surrounding events of that night, and the conclusions that I have drawn. I have examined the various contemporary newspaper reports, the newspaper series from the 1950s and the subsequent book and television show ("Not Proven") from the 1980s. I have applied my little local knowledge and managed to dig a little deeper on some facts with the modern tools that we now have available, such as the internet and microfiche. The result is my theory that may well be disproved by a more capable or thorough investigator at a later date.

With over 100 years hindsight, and a far greater understanding of human nature than was ever available to the Edwardians, we may come to a seemingly obvious conclusion that most certainly could not have been so clear in those early days. As such, no inference should be made of any suggestion of incompetence on the part of those early police.

The 1857 Police Scotland Act had established separate police forces in towns, burghs and counties. This meant that policing was very much a local matter - policemen were usually very well informed about and connected to their local communities. Perhaps the notion of the local "bobby" was to die later with PC Dixon of Dock Green, but in the earliest days of the force, an ever-present authority who could call on additional local resources as required undertook crime prevention.

Above – An Ayrshire bobby from 1910, PC Number 140 complete with his six-panel hat and ambulance badge on the right hand sleeve.

When the Portencross murder took place in 1913, officers came to assist from Largs, Dalry, Ardrossan, and even as far away as Ayr. Indeed, Ardrossan had been established as a Burgh and so maintained its own police force. This case came under the direct jurisdiction of District in the County Constabulary, and so Inspector Grant of Largs was listed as the lead investigator.

National newspapers descended on the scene of the murder. Curiously, however, the most detailed crime descriptions came from the local newspaper entitled the Ardrossan & Saltcoats Herald – and these notes will ultimately give us the most significant clues. The Largs and Millport Weekly News reports were considerably shorter and erroneous in some cases, but also useful.

The police officers were, as we might nowadays regard, local community officers. Many were largely there to simply offer a helping hand to the public. There were little or no central resources to be drawn upon as we might nowadays expect, such as a forensic lab. Indeed, even fingerprint analysis was still in its most early development.

Burgh and County Police Constabularies operated independently of each other, but frequently co-operated on matters of importance. At the time of this murder, West Kilbride had its own Police station manned twenty-four hours a day by one Sergeant and various Constables. Local police stations, under the guidance of the Town Council, could also deputise citizens if appropriate, and this was occasionally done for inspections by

County to make the station look busier or more efficient.

Above – West Kilbride Police Station in the 1970's

Outside of inspections, local rural Police were notoriously lazy, ill-trained and seriously under-equipped. Despite telephones being fairly commonplace in many businesses and middle-class houses in 1913, the West Kilbride County Constabulary was yet to benefit from this new technology.

From the 1870s onwards, West Kilbride was an incredibly popular tourist destination. This had likely peaked around 1906, but even in 1913 you could expect upwards of 10,000 people to be staying at the various lodgings, homes and hotels in the village each weekend. Portencross was a very popular walking and exploring destination.

A frequent charabanc bus would ferry visitors from the town centre to the tiny village where there was a small post office, boarding house, farm and of course the castle.

October - the month of the murder - was certainly in the low season, so the town would not be expecting the highest volumes of visitors. Even so, following the murder there were rumours of strange men in the village and heated discussions The crime rate was very low in West Kilbride. Holidaymakers to this village were generally those in employment. Those on sick leave, or on holiday from work occupied the large local convalescent and co-operative homes. Also nearby was the Seamill Hydropathic Hotel, which was not an inexpensive holiday. This had been established in 1886 and catered for the middle and upper classes who would seek solace and recuperation through a strict regime of water-based treatments and rest.

One of the misconstructions of the crime (as evidenced in the 1955 story by Glasgow Journalist Jack House) is to describe the location of Portencross as remote, quiet, and lonely. This was not entirely the case in 1913, although it had become so by the 1950s. A simple glance through the 1911 Census shows how many families were living in bothies, farm outbuildings, and agricultural cottages all around the area. Often

14

times, there were nine or ten families living in a single room. Even in the Auchenames estate, there were gardeners and lodgers in the farm cottages.

Regardless of the weather, at 8:30pm on a Saturday night there could be a reasonable number of people wandering about the beautiful area. Any potential assassin might expect to be observed and figure this into their plans, perhaps waiting for the cover of darkness to commit the crime.

North Bank cottage lies on a farm path where to the south is the tiny clachan of Portencross and to the north the path would ultimately take the traveller to the slightly larger village of Fairlie. The first stop on this track would have been Fences Farm, the home of dairyman Thomas Muir (44) and his wife (42). Together they had three sons and six daughters. The oldest son was 19 and the oldest daughter 17, and all of the children worked on the farm or attended school. They also had a servant living with them, 21-year old Maggie Carron.

At Goldenberry Farm, Neil Black (37) and his wife Annie (40) had three sons and three daughters all at school. Goldenberry bothy, on the farm, housed John McCrae (42), Barbra McCrae (40) and a boarder Patrick Murphy (40) who had come from Ireland to work on the farms.

In Lobster Cottage, there was Thomas Malcolm (67) a retired fisherman, his wife Margaret (61), daughter Jeanie (32) who was a stationers assistant, son Thomas (26) who was a joiner, Ann Simpson (54) a widow housewife, her daughter Jeanie (20) a dressmaker, son James (20) also a joiner, and son William (11) who attended school. Also in that cottage were two boarders – Fergus Nicol (30) and Robert West (18) who were listed as painters.

The Portencross Dairy had a similar number as did West Cottage. Four adults who were related occupied the small village Post Office.

Therefore, as we can see, in the early part of a fateful Saturday evening it is highly unlikely that the village would have been so lonely or quiet. Several people would have likely been milling about, if only to get away from such cramped conditions.

Victims of crime tended to be through alcoholic misadventure rather than deliberate acts of wanton destruction. Deaths did occur under strange conditions, such as bodies being found on the long coastline, but never through murder - more rather through taking strong drink and falling asleep in cold conditions.

Of course, the newspapers told stories of violence in the cities, especially when such tales included details of knife or gun crimes. A thirst for salacious detail was developing as a result of the new mass circulation of reading materials such as through the subscription library on the Main Street of West Kilbride. As we shall see, it might be reasonable that people living in very remote circumstances should own a gun for protection – especially, for example, if they had knowledge of shootings in Glasgow city.

My own family lived at the south end of Portencross at the time of the murder. My father had not yet been adopted into the Brown family, but his adoptive mother and father had arrived in their youth in the 1890s to take up positions in service at one of the larger houses of Ardneil. The Brown children - William, Alistair and Margaret were all born in the early 20th Century and were attending school in 1913.

Much later, in the 1970s, a revolver was found in a nearby field. Local police questioned my grandmother and father to see if they knew anything that might shed light on the murder, for she had not been questioned at the time. She knew nothing of course, and within a few days the revolver was confirmed to be from the World War II era. Why my grandmother was never questioned at the time of the murder remains a mystery, although it may shed a tiny light on the investigation with respect to how the murder investigation was directed.

I believe that the police had suspected one particular man from a fairly early stage of the investigation, but that perhaps he had an alibi. In the days that followed the murder, West Kilbride was certainly in frenzy. Uncertainty seemed to beget sorrow when six days after the murder the beloved Minister of the village Church of Scotland, Reverend John Lamb, died suddenly, albeit of natural causes. He had retired to his bed some two weeks earlier complaining of heart pains, and subsequently died of heart failure.

West Kilbride is a very insular village, being surrounded by eleven hills and the sea. During the police investigation, rumours were spreading of strange men walking in the village at night. It seemed the whole area was a greenhouse of gossip regarding the case. This did not make the job of the police any easier as they were to be found racing after suggested illusory suspects or searching for clues at the suggestion of another member of the public. Meanwhile as time passed, any evidence left by the real killer would have been harder and harder to find.

The gentlemen of the press also descended in

18

their droves. From the national to the local, journalists were sent to West Kilbride to describe the scene as investigations progressed. In those days it was rare for the syndication of news stories, and so each newspaper sent their own journalist. One newspaper, having failed to get a picture of the police at the scene of the crime, staged a shot by using a postman in his uniform to pose as if he were a policeman standing guard at North Bank Cottage. This photograph was used as a postcard image and sold in its thousands throughout the area - such was the level of gossip and interest in the mysterious Portencross murder. I have this original postcard in my own collection and have put it on the cover of this book.

Of course, as we now know, no person was ever charged with the murder. At one point in the investigation, the police were so certain of a suspect in Glasgow that they announced to the press that an arrest was imminent. That arrest strangely came to nothing and no explanation was ever given. Without the police file, we are not likely to find out what had happened with this suspicion. I believe that the police investigators had a strong inclination as to the identity of the killer - as did Alexander McLaren - but neither could provide the needed evidence to secure a conviction.

So, the question stands: how much of our understanding of these mysterious events was steered by the press? Let us take, for example, the generation-later writings of the well-known and respected Glasgow journalist, Jack House. In 1955, House wrote a daily series of articles on the Portencross Murder. These articles were published every day for a week in the Glasgow Evening News. The source information for this series, later book and television show came from only one single source - the Glasgow Herald.

Neither the original Herald journalists, Jack House, Alexander McLaren nor indeed myself ever saw the police file on the investigation. All the information that we have comes from the newspapers and the speculation surrounding subsequent events.

These works of Jack House explained the practicalities of the crime, the methods used and the opportunity as it presented itself to the murderer, but he was unable to determine the motive. Without the motive, it looked like the case would never be solved.

In 1983, another generation later, House published a book and presented a TV show ("Not Proven") that restated the original analysis of that single journalistic source, the Glasgow Herald. The show did not come to any new conclusions;

however, it introduced the mystery to a new generation and brought publicity to the inconclusive police investigation.

In this book, I have gone back through the original newspaper sources from all the journalists that attended the murder scene. In doing so, I have discovered a number of inaccuracies reported in the regional newspapers that shed possible new light on the case. I have also been able to use my local knowledge to a limited extent, to develop the events as they unfolded on the night of the murder and in the subsequent days of the investigation.

The following chapters will develop my own theory as to the motive and the murderer, and present a new case for both. Without sight of the police file, my musings can only remain as theory, but I do hope that any further discussions may finally shed greater light on the terrible events of October 1913.

In terms of the spelling of names in this book, I have tried to adopt a pragmatic approach. By 1913, the area had become more commonly known as Portencross, whereas prior to the 20th Century the village was known as Portincross and the area where North Bank was situated was called Pencross. The journalists of the Largs and Millport Weekly News, presumably being more traditional, used the older spelling in their articles, whereas the Ardrossan & Saltcoats Herald, being more contemporary, used the new spelling of Portencross. I have given a short explanation of the two names through history in Appendix 1.

Similarly, North Bank Cottage was most commonly referred to in three words in 1913, but there are occasional references to Northbank as one word in some articles such as the Ardrossan & Saltcoats Herald. In this instance, I have decided to use the original spelling as it was in more common usage in 1913.

The West Kilbride medical practitioner is variously referred to as Dr Mure and Dr More. Mure certainly is a well-known ancient family name in these parts, but the spelling of More is used more often in the literature. I have therefore decided to use the spelling More. If there are any people affected by this choice, I apologise.

Finally, I have been unable to find any living descendent of my proposed murderer, but in the event that one or more should see this book, I would apologise for any offence I may cause in making my thoughts known.

Stephen Brown, April 2018

CHAPTER 1: Murder Most Foul

It was on the evening of the 18th of October 1913 that the fatal shots were fired. Bullets hit all three occupants of the tiny living room, and 49-year old Mary Gunn lay dead from a shot to the heart. An unknown assailant had fired six shots through a tiny window of the little cottage before escaping into the night, never to be captured or even identified.

Above – Alexander McLaren

North Bank Cottage

North Bank Cottage, situated on a peninsula on the southwest coast of Scotland, was (and indeed is to this day) a remote farm cottage, some one thousand yards north of the nearest neighbour in the tiny clachan or village known as Portencross. To the north of the cottage lay farming land and the Hunterston Estate, the nearest house being Fences Farm about a mile away. Behind the cottage lie steep cliffs, known locally as the three sisters, and to the west lies the firth of the river Clyde. Between the river and the cottage is a farm path. Again, half a mile distant is the clachan shown in the map at the start of this book.

Above – North Bank Cottage as it is nowadays, set against the backdrop of the cliffs above

On the 25th October 1913, The Ardrossan &
Saltcoats Herald gave an excellent description of
the surrounds of the Cottage - it follows:

> *Northbank is beautifully situated. Lonely it
> certainly is, for the nearest dwelling on
> one hand is at Portincross, nearly half a
> mile away, while on the other there is no
> house nearer than the farm of Fences on
> the Hunterston Estate, distant a good mile.
> Not everyone would choose an abode so
> slightly favourable to social intercourse,
> but the charm of the surroundings is
> unquestionable. The cottage stands in the
> middle of a bay of which the southern
> extremity is the ridge of rocks jutting into
> the sea at Portincross, a ridge which rises
> abruptly from the shore, and, but for a five
> gap through which a farm cart passes, cuts
> off the hamlet from the bay beyond. Semi
> circles go back from the rocky shore, a
> line of cliffs encloses a stretch of flat land
> on the inland side, and Northbank Cottage
> is built close up to the cliff foot, almost at
> the central point of the curve. The sea is
> distant about three hundred yards. Behind
> the house a sheer precipice, ivy clad and
> bearing here and there a mountain ash,
> rises to a height of 150 feet. At some points
> to the side the rock is turf-clad, and not so*

perpendicular, and may easily be climbed, but the whole place is covered with a tangle of fern and bracken, hawthorn, briar and brambles. On the Portincross (the south) side of the cottage is a patch of garden, enclosed by wire sitting about four feet high, supported on light stakes.

Such is the scene of the crime.

Alexander McLaren and the Gunn Family

By May 1913, 60-year old Alexander McLaren and his 61 years old wife, Jessie, had rented North Bank cottage. They had quickly made a few friends already in the tiny village.

We are not told where McLaren was born, merely that he had arrived in Ayrshire in his youth when he took up a position of managing an ironware and hardware store at Barkip in Dalry. There he met his wife to be, who was the eldest daughter of three to Gilbert Gunn. Gunn was a railway contractor and would be contender for the title of strongest man in Scotland. Gunn and his wife lived at Burnside in Beith, and his company was engaged in many large-scale railway works in the area throughout the middle of the 19th Century.

Mary Gunn, our murder victim, was the youngest of Gilbert's daughters. In 1883 Gilbert died, and

Mary took a job as the first telephone operator in Beith. In her youth, Mary was a renowned beauty, having been suggested as a possible beauty queen. This fact was later to be considered in relation to a potential motive for her murder.

The middle sister Eliza married and immigrated to Saskatchewan in Canada, whilst Jessie and Alexander (now married) purchased a bakery business in Port William, Wigtownshire. Over the next few years Alexander and Jessie built the bakery business whilst Mary was promoted to manageress of the Ardrossan Telephone Exchange.

Alexander and Jessie owned a bakery in Port William for over 20 years. Towards the end of that time Mary and her mother moved to help in the business, but sadly her mother passed away after only a year or two. Then, Alexander and Jessie purchased a sheep farm in Taynuilt in Perthshire and left Mary to manage down the original business towards an ultimate sale or closure. Mary was recorded in the business rates valuation roll in 1905 and so was still there in that year.

By character and belief, Alexander McLaren was an evangelical Christian. He built an Ebenezer Mission Hall in the village whilst farming in Taynuilt. It seems from the little that we know of the events surrounding the murder that his evangelical faith may have slackened somewhat in his later life to be less extreme over the character of others.

Above – Jessie McLaren

Mary Gunn

Following the closure of the bakery business in Port William, Mary decided to visit her sister Eliza, who with her husband John Craig now lived in Saskatchewan, Canada. On her departure, there was every expectation that she might emigrate fully. After she initially settled in Canada, she met a young man and briefly formed

28

a romantic attachment, but this was not to last. During the investigations, police made enquiry of this young man, only to find that he was most definitely in Canada on the night of the murder.

Whilst in Canada, Mary wrote to Alexander and her sister about how unhappy she was. Alexander invited her to return home to Scotland and to stay with them, when he retired.

And so it was, shortly after the failed Canadian romance, Mary returned to Scotland to take up residence with her older sister and husband at North Bank. In the winter of 1912/13 Alexander had decided to retire. The farm was to be sold and the animals were auctioned off during the spring and summer of 1913. Whilst this process was ongoing, Alexander, his wife and her sister rented the secluded cottage at North Bank.

The Murder

It is by stealth that the killer approached the south side of that lonely cottage. According to McLaren's later statement (corroborated by his wife), the time was around 8:30pm. It was pitch dark outside, and there were light sprinklings of rain. One newspaper had claimed that it was very stormy and rainy, but I suspect this can be attributed to the trends of sensational writing of the time.

DOMESTIC SERVANTS,

EXPERIENCED MEN

(Single and Married),

.. AND ..

INEXPERIENCED MEN

(Single),

WANTED FOR CANADA.

Full Particulars regarding

WAGES, ASSISTED PASSAGES, &c.,

.. AT ..

SIMPSONS' AGENCY,

38 MAIN STREET, LARGS.

AMERICAN and CANADIAN DOLLARS

and other Foreign and Colonial Money

☞ EXCHANGED. ☜

Above – An advertisement in the local press for men and women to go to Canada. Absolutely coincidentally, Alexander McLaren borrowed a book from the public subscription library in Simpsons, West Kilbride, which he was reading on the night of the murder.

The three occupants of the little living room were gathered around the fire whilst Alexander McLaren read from W.W. Jacob's latest book. McLaren's later statements seem to conflict, as he stated to one newspaper that he had just started reading when the first shot rang out, and to another that he had read four chapters. He also claimed the book had been chosen by Mary and that he had borrowed it himself from the library. I can find no significance in these errors in relation to the crime.

The detailed reports in the Ardrossan & Saltcoats Herald are most helpful. They reported that the fireplace faced in the direction of the sea - to the west. McLaren was positioned to the right-hand side of it, sitting in his high back armchair, with the book in his right hand and his left hand resting in the arm being the only part of him visible to the murderer.

Jessie was in the middle of the three. She sat facing towards the fire, knitting. Mary was to the left-hand side, where she would have been able to view out the window and up the path towards the tiny village. There was a table in the room upon which sat a small table lamp, which may have obstructed the view of the approach of the murderer.

The following picture is taken from the

Ardrossan & Saltcoats Herald newspaper report in 1913. It shows the relative positions of the three in the room, the table and the fireside. This is not drawn to scale.

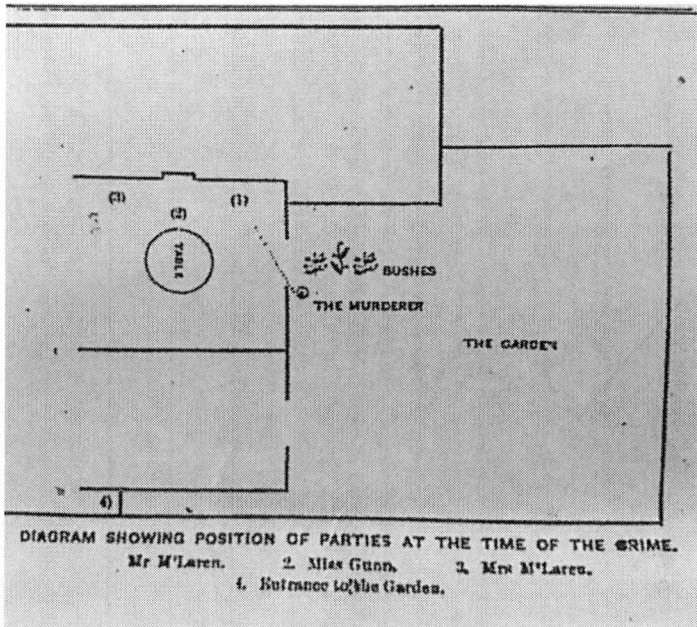

DIAGRAM SHOWING POSITION OF PARTIES AT THE TIME OF THE CRIME.
Mr M'Laren.   2. Miss Gunn.   3. Mrs M'Laren.
4. Entrance to the Garden.

Interestingly, we are told that despite the wind and rain, the blinds of the little sitting room remained open. Was this so that Mary could observe? And who would approach this rural scene of tranquillity?

Reportedly, there were two dogs kept either in the outhouse or loose in the yard – a collie and an eight-month old terrier puppy. As the murderer approached, they did not bark. Perhaps the rain and wind had softened the sound of the oncoming intruder, or is it possible that they would have known the smell and sound of the killer?

There are considerable differences in report as to the exact movements during the shooting, and as to the final destination of the individual bullets. The following is my best interpretation of the various accounts.

McLaren was reading when a shot rang out, shattering the lowest left pane of eight in the window. That first bullet removed the tip of McLaren's left index finger right down to the bone and apparently (Largs and Millport Weekly News) then went through the book he was reading.

Before Alexander McLaren could understand or react to what had just happened, a second and third shot rang out. The second bullet was found embedded in the arm of his high-backed armchair, and the third was only later recovered in the padding of the back.

One later writer in the 1950s claimed that Jessie had seen the assassin smash the pane of the window with the muzzle of the gun, but I suspect that this is simply dramatic embellishment from when gangster and western matinees had gripped the public imagination. There was no mention of this in the original statement by McLaren. Smashing the window and alerting the occupants of the small room would seem somewhat counter-productive to the attempted murder.

The following was the reported statement of Alexander McLaren, the day after the murder:

"After we had tea we made everything comfortable in the sitting-room. I was at one side of the fire, with a book of W.W. Jacobs in my hand, reading. My wife was seated opposite, and beside her was Miss Gunn. They were both knitting, and I read the book aloud. They laughed heartily at Jacobs' humour, and we were as happy as can be.

"About half-past eight, when I had read three or four chapters of the story, we were suddenly frightened by the report of a revolver shot close in at the window.
"Miss Gunn rose to come to my side. While she was in the act she was struck by a bullet and fell on the fender. "Oh Alex, I am shot," were the last words that she said.

"My wife was also struck by a bullet, and she fell into my arms. While I was

attending to her, I cried "floor, floor, Mary," intending that they should crouch to avoid the shots. It was then I discovered that my own hand was covered with blood, the top of my left index finger being shattered.

"Whoever fired the shots must have been close in at the window, they sounded so near. The blinds were not drawn. It was not our custom to draw them, since nobody comes about the place at night."

Note that McLaren says "*...a revolver shot close in at the window.*" This may indicate that the police had told him that the gun was a revolver fired from close to the side of the window. This is repeated in the last paragraph as if to emphasise. He also draws attention to the fact that the blinds were not drawn, as supposedly was their custom.

We now know from the scene of the crime that three shots were fired at McLaren, two embedded in the seat and the third piercing through his book, having taken off the top of his finger and ended embedded in the wall.

Next, the attention of the foul murderer turned to the far side of the room where poor Mary Gunn had jumped up. We believe now that a fourth shot was aimed at Mary, which struck Jessie McLaren in the back just above the kidneys. A fifth shot struck Mary's body (we are not told where) and the sixth and final shot pierced her heart fatally.

The newspaper stated that Alexander sought to cover his wife with his own body and only then noticed that he himself had been wounded in the hand, as blood dripped to the floor. He also said that he had crouched behind his seat between the first and second shots.

As silent as their approach, the shooter then made their escape into the dark, never to be seen again or identified.

The aftermath of the murder unfolded many events that, to our modern eye, may seem as strange as the killing itself. As silence reigned, Alexander McLaren rose to his feet. In front of him his sister-in-law lay dead and bleeding, and his wife, shot in the back, was slumped to the floor.

There is little mention in the ensuing reports of McLaren's reaction to the devastating before him, or of any action he may have made to secure the safety of his wife. We are told that he stopped to remove his slippers and put on his boots before he ran outside to chase the killer. Having briefly looked around, he went to the barn where the two dogs were kept and loosed them to seek out any sign of the intruder. Again, there is an inconsistency in these accounts, as he later also suggested that the dogs were already roaming outside.

The police later compared his own boot pattern with this found in the wet soil outside in the night – they did not match. The police never stated that they tried to match his slippers to the boot prints in the garden, but we shall assume that they did.

Is it not strange to us that McLaren's first instincts in the minutes after the shooting were not to look after his wife? Or even to secure the property from further attack or robbery, but to chase after an unknown and dangerous attacker, in the pitch dark?

Apparently, he did not know the motive of the killer and supposed it might be robbery, and yet he ran outside, leaving the door open. Later, his wife was to confirm her own anxiety as to whether or not the killer might return. What was McLaren expecting to happen if the dogs had caught up to the evildoer? It seems to me that if the murderer had been caught, then surely there could have been further violence.

It is purely a conjecture on my part, but I believe that McLaren thought he knew whom the murderer might be. He had expected to run outside, to confront and confirm the identity of this mysterious person, and perhaps take revenge upon him or at least overpower him until he could be presented to the authorities. The reasoning behind my conjecture will come from my analysis of McLaren's central role in subsequent events. I do not, however, hold to Jack House's theory that McLaren had a sinister part in the murder.

We are not told how long Alexander searched for the killer with the dogs, but the doctor who was to pronounce Mary dead did not arrive from the village of West Kilbride until some 45 to 48 minutes after the shooting. Taking into account the actions of McLaren, it is reasonable to suggest that the dogs were used for at least ten to fifteen minutes before he ran for help.

It is imperative to remember that the scene was pitch dark and rainy. If the killer had turned north, I think it highly unlikely that he would have made his escape so cleanly without detection by the dogs, or ultimately the police. Likewise, I do not think that the dogs would have ignored a figure hiding in the rocks at the seashore. One local later suggested that the perpetrator may have committed suicide in the sea after the crime, but no body was ever found.

There also was the suggestion that the killer had

climbed the cliffs behind the cottage, but this does sound rather far-fetched and would have been most inconvenient to the murderer trying to make good a simple escape.

It is my humble opinion that the killer must have already escaped to safety in the nearby village, or that he was known to the dogs by scent. With no luck in his initial searches, McLaren went back into the cottage, left his wife alone with her dead sister and ran up the farm path towards the village of Portencross.

There are two slightly different versions of what McLaren did next. One version has McLaren run the length of the farm path and then turn left to approach the farm. On raising the alarm at the farmhouse, he and fellow farmer Alexander Murray went to the Laird of Auchenames manor where there was a telephone. In 1913 West Kilbride Police Station was not equipped with a telephone, so the Laird telephoned a friend in the village who promptly raised the alarm with the police and rural practitioner Dr More. According to all later reports, McLaren and Murray returned to the farm path near to Shore Boarding House where he met a taxi carrying two local policemen and Doctor More. The car then drove the entire party to North Bank Cottage.

I am not convinced by this rather clumsy version

of events. There is a gate in the wall to the Auchenames Estate, very close to the end of the Pier (as shown on the map in the beginning of this book), and I believe it more likely that McLaren would first have entered there.

This is the second version of events - that McLaren entered the estate by the gateway and ran to the Laird's house whereupon the alarm was raised. Whilst the police and doctor were being raised in West Kilbride, McLaren ran along a footpath to the nearby Portencross Farm to tell his friends, Alexander Murray and his wife, and to get further help. Mrs Murray answered the door and McLaren garbled "They're all shot at my house, my wife and Miss Gunn are lying shot on the floor". Murray came down to see what the commotion was, and he and McLaren then returned to the Laird's house, presumably to be told that the police were on their way. This was about 9pm. Then they both went down the path to the farm pathway at which point they met the taxi outside Shore Boarding House.

It was 30 minutes from when McLaren ran out of North Bank until the message had reached the police station and a taxi had arrived, according to the police. The taxi driver claimed he drove down to Portencross in 8 minutes, with a pause to pick up McLaren (2 minutes) and a further 8 minutes to then drive down the rocky farm path to North

Bank.

As I mentioned earlier, I believe that McLaren had a suspicion as to the identity of the killer, and I note that he took this circuitous route avoiding the main Portencross thoroughfare until he was accompanied.

On arrival at the scene, one account suggests that Jessie had managed to pull herself to her feet and was standing over the dead body of her sister. The local newspaper, however, claimed she had been lying alongside the dead body of her sister for the entire period her husband had gone, and was found there on arrival. According to Jessie, nobody had attempted entry to the cottage whilst McLaren had been away. Doctor More recorded the death of Mary Gunn a little after 9:15pm – perhaps some 45-48 minutes after the shooting.

The following day, Dr More was to comment to the press that Mary Gunn's body was already cold when he had arrived at the scene. Normally we would not expect a dead body to reach room temperature until some three hours after death had occurred, but the fact that Mary had been lying on a stone floor for the entire 48 minutes was deemed to explain this apparent discrepancy (Largs & Millport News).

Certainly, in the earliest hours of this mystery,

one public theory was that McLaren himself might have had some nefarious purpose in the enactment of the crime. This was certainly a considered opinion of Jack House in 1955, but it would have required either a serious memory lapse or the collaboration of his wife Jessie. It seems a little unlikely given the subsequent events of 1914 and the slander court trial, to be explained below.

Immediately on arrival, the police sought to secure the scene of the crime and gather any evidence they could. Due to the mysterious nature of this crime, the rural location, and the huge national public interest that was to follow, many individual pieces of evidence from the scene were reported in the press. We may not have the police file, but we can discuss this evidence in some depth in the hope that now, some 105 years later, we can finally establish who killed Mary Gunn.

CHAPTER 2: Crime Scene Investigation

On arrival at the scene of the crime, the West Kilbride County Constabulary police officers attempted to save any evidence that they could. As Doctor More attended to the wounds of Jessie and Alexander McLaren, and pronounced Mary Gunn dead, the police officers searched the house. They immediately recognised that the windowpane had been shattered and some pieces of the frame had been damaged in the incident. Fragments of glass were mainly pushed inside the house, with only one tiny fragment lying outside, presumably recoiled shattering.

The window nowadays appears to be about three feet from the ground. The shooter might therefore be pointing at a height of about 3.5 feet. However, examination of the photographs from 1913 suggests that the ground level was slightly lower then than appears now, and I have estimated that the windowpane height was around 4-4.5 feet. The average Victorian man was five foot and five inches and the average woman five foot. Therefore, it is reasonable to suggest that the murderer could have crouched down to fire through the windowpane.

Even in the darkness, the West Kilbride police

thought that they could discern six distinct footmarks described later in the newspapers as boot prints. Two of the boot prints were found outside to the left of the little window, right beside the wall. The police immediately compared the size of the boot prints to McLaren's boots and noted they did not fit. This indicated that the shooter had aimed the gun through the window at a very sharp angle.

We do have a detailed description of the scene by the window from the Ardrossan & Saltcoats Herald on the week of the murder:

> *"The window in one of eight panes, of which only one - that in the bottom left-hand corner (looking from outside) -was broken. Innumerable fragments of glass lay inside the room while only one small piece was found outside. Immediately outside, a hole had been dug in the soil some time earlier in order to reach the drain, and the soil was heaped up at the side of the cavity. A tree had grown close to the wall, but had been cut, leaving about five feet of the stump, the base quite close to the wall with the rest sloping upward and outward. Obviously the murderer had stood close against the wall to the left, a position from which he could only see Mr McLaren, unless he leant*

44

forward to see further into the room. A footmark was visible in the soft ground at this point, and the bark of the tree stump is abraded some inches above the ground as if a heavy boot had scraped it. On the wall close to the left margin of the window there is a smear of smoke and a stone is chipped. On the right angle wall to the right hand side of the window, the lime wash is also chipped, and the fact that a bullet was found under this latter mark seems to indicate that one of the shots struck the stonework at the window, ricocheted across to the other side of the angle and fell to the ground. Another shot has cut a clean semi circle out of the wooden astragal of the window. Taking into account the position in which the murderer stood or knelt, and the respective positions of the occupants of the sitting room, two facts become clear. The first is that it was Mr McLaren that was aimed at, and the second is the person who fired the shots was not only accustomed to handling a revolver, but was something of a marksman."

Inspector Grant of Largs Police examined the footprint pattern on the night of the murder. Next to the window were two reasonably clear boot prints. Further down the path he found four indistinct footprints that were unusable. He had officers place a basket over the two prints to protect them until plaster of Paris could be supplied for impressions to be made.

The Ardrossan & Saltcoats Herald was later to report that the police had found the footprints to be "Holsted" boots with a three-basket logo on the sole. This was a misprint and the boots were of the "Halstead" design which was a precursor to what we now know as Chelsea boots i.e. ankle length boots usually worn by women but occasionally by men. From the imprint, we realise that the boots were flat soled and new enough to not be worn away enough to ensure the logo could be clearly determined. These boots would form a huge part of the public speculation over the coming weeks.

The Bullet

In the morning after the murder, a seventh, unspent bullet was found on the ground below the right-hand side of the window. As the bullet was fully intact, it was examined by the police and checked against the shells used by McLaren. They did not match.

There was also a rather sensational claim in the newspaper report that the gunman was something of a marksman. Various newspapers repeated this sensation, and indeed, a senior policeman stated that the sheer number of bullets fired seemed to suggest a professional killer.

However, despite three shots being fired at close range, no direct hit was made. An indirect hit was made on the person of Jessie McLaren, and I am therefore forced to consider that the fatal shot to Mary Gunn may have been more accidental than by design.

As we know, the murderer had approached the cottage without alarming the dogs, suggesting a level of familiarity. The criminal took great care to stay close to the side of the wall, even where there were tree stumps as obstruction, so as not to be seen. The main reason for this could be so that they might not be recognised. With the benefit of hindsight, we now know that in 79% of murders, the victim knows the perpetrator (Uniform Crime Reporting Program of the FBI, 2011).

The local newspaper concluded that the primary target was Alexander McLaren, and certainly he was the victim of three deliberate shots from the outset. However, as the killer approached from beside the wall, McLaren would have been the only person initially visible. Even if the killer had another target in mind, they would certainly have to neutralise McLaren first as the primary defence in any scenario of violence. Three shots were fired at McLaren, rather than all six. Had the shooter not known the little family, and perhaps if robbery was indeed the motive, logic might dictate that the assassin should use all six bullets in the attempt to kill McLaren. Therefore, it does not necessarily follow that the primary target was Alexander McLaren.

The Largs and Millport Weekly News made comment that after the first burst of three shots, the small sitting room had become filled with smoke. This is entirely possible as the wind would have been rushing inward, and the bullets were propelled by cordite that does generate considerable smoke when fired.

The second burst of gunshot was loosed in the direction of Mary Gunn. One wide shot injured Jessie McLaren (possibly due to the amount of smoke now in the room), a second then hit and injured Mary Gunn and the third was the fatal shot that tore through her heart. Could it be that McLaren was not in fact the target of this heinous crime, but simply obstructive in its successful commission?

Why did the killer fire all six shots through only one tiny windowpane? The conclusions that I draw from this fact are that all six shots were fired quickly, and probably in two bursts of three. As the intended targets (McLaren and Gunn) jumped out of their seats after the initial shots, there little time was to be lost. A change in angle was perhaps not the most effective use of the remaining time whilst the targets were in view.

As we consider this, we may be tempted to think that this murder was the work of a seasoned assassin, but in the flurry of the moment, instinct or panic might well have taken over an amateur shooter and they might well come to the same course of action.

Of course, we ought to discount the possibility that there was more than one murderer, as only six bullets were fired and only one set of footprints were found immediately after the murder. We might also consider that the shooter was not experienced in handling small firearms, although we shall explore this conclusion further below, when we consider the bullets used in the commission of the crime.

The Escape

Next, the murderer made their escape. As aforementioned, the area was dark and somewhat sombre. We might conclude that the assassin had planned somewhere to disappear to, or at least had knowledge of the area. Once again, the collie dog and puppy were unalarmed. Could it have followed that the murderer lived locally? For then they would have had a place to hide very quickly after the assassination.

There is no mention in any newspapers of police conducting door-to-door questioning immediately after the crime. As mentioned above, none of my ancestors were interviewed. Such a failure in detection methodology might have given a local killer time to dispose of the weapon and the boots that had made the footprints, or to cover any remaining tracks.

The Weapon

As aforementioned, six bullets were fired, and a seventh unspent bullet was found in the ground. These were compared against McLaren's own shotgun. There was evidence that his shotgun had been fired in the recent past, and on questioning McLaren informed police that he had been out shooting rabbits that very day. The seventh bullet did not match McLaren's shotgun.

The police concluded that the murder weapon was a heavy revolver of the 'Colt' type, as might be used in army service or for small arm protection. Nowadays each bullet would of course be tested for fingerprints, but there was no such technique in 1913 that would have allowed this. Fingerprint evidence had been used in criminal investigations since 1902 and in murders since 1905, but there was no established technique for the collection and analysis of such evidence. This would not be seriously considered until after the First World War.

Colt guns were sold in Britain in the early part of the century, but a similar manufacture was the British made 'Webley'. Bullets from either gun would fit the other. The police specified the calibre of the weapon used in the commission of the crime to be around .450. The image below shows the shapes of the various Webley gun bullets.

The Webley Mark III had larger flat nose bullets which may have been initially mistaken for a shotgun bullet when the crime scene bullets were compared to the shells used in McLaren's shotgun. However, authorities found the Mark III to be in contravention of the Hague Convention in the amount of damage this kind of revolver could do, and it was withdrawn to be replaced in 1912 by the Mark IV.

As the Webley Mark 3 bullets were flat nosed, they were slower in speed after firing and caused a little less damage on impact. This matches the injuries to McLaren and his wife who fully recovered from being shot. The fatal shot to Mary Gunn however was a direct hit to the heart.

Both types bullets used cordite propellant that

would account for the smoke damage seen on the white walls of the cottage. However, after such a length of time since the crime, we may never know which exact model of gun killed Mary Gunn.

In attempting to discover the name of the murderer, we must consider how they might have come by their firearm, and for what original purpose it had been intended. It was fairly commonplace in the Edwardian age for gentlemen to purchase their own Webley firearm, and many ex-servicemen would have owned one. It does not necessarily follow that the killer was a gentleman of considerable means, or an ex-serviceman, but merely that they had connection enough to access a gun of this type.

Shooting, particularly hunting, was an extremely common pastime in the early 20th Century. In the Ardrossan & Saltcoats Herald of the week of the murder, I counted four separate advertisements for shotgun cartridges including our very own local Nobels Explosives. This suggests rather a high demand in the area.

It may seem rather insensitive with our modern values, but in the days following the murder (despite the massive publicity and extensive searches being conducted throughout the Portencross peninsula and surrounding countryside) Lieutenant Colonel Hunter-Weston held a shooting party on the Hunterston estate. Similarly did Mr Graham of the Crosbie Estate. On both days the press reported - "the bags were fair".

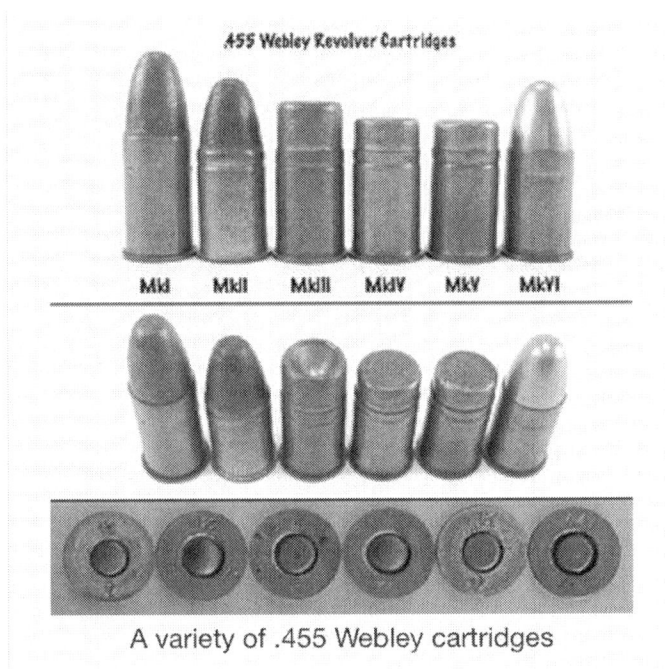

.455 Webley Revolver Cartridges

MkI MkII MkIII MkIV MkV MkVI

A variety of .455 Webley cartridges

Above – the various types of Webley bullets available. In common circulation at the time of the murder would have been the Mark III and Mark IV (the two centre bullets shown)

Above – One of the many advertisements in the local papers for shotgun cartridges. Nowadays it is hard to believe just how many people owned and fired guns in the countryside.

Police were now fully aware of the method of murder and the opportunity that had presented itself to the killer. Over the next one hundred and five years, the fruitless search would continue to explore the motive behind the appalling murder. In due course, I will make my own suggestion as to who killed Mary Gunn.

CHAPTER 3: The Search

The murder had taken place around 8:30pm on the Saturday night. Within a few hours, several policemen had arrived from Largs including Inspector Grant who was the ranking Police Officer for the district. Grant was to remain at the scene all week. By one thirty in the morning an Inspector stationed at Ardrossan arrived with some of his men, followed quickly by Superintendent McCreath of Dalry Station and even more men. As first light dawned, the search for evidence began along the coast.

Above from the left – On the Monday following the murder, Inspector Grant of Largs, Chief Constable Robertson-Glasgow and Alexander McLaren (with his injured finger in a sling).

On Sunday morning, the Procurator Fiscal and the Sheriff arrived on the scene at North Bank – which had now become a command centre for the police investigation.

The Day of the Crime

During the night, West Kilbride medic Dr More had dressed Jessie's and Alexander's wounds. Neither of the two could shed any light on the motive for the murder. When interviews were later being given to the press by McLaren he placed a great deal of emphasis on the notion that the shooter was a man. He also claimed that his wife might have glimpsed the man at the window.

McLaren was able to recount the events of the previous day prior to the murder. He had risen in the morning and after breakfast, had gone north with his two dogs on the isolated peninsula, shooting rabbits. He returned home sometime in the afternoon, having successfully caught one rabbit. The rabbit remained in the kitchen awaiting preparation.

The next part of the day remains a little mysterious but does give us an insight into the motive behind the dreadful deed. Mary had walked into West Kilbride to go shopping. At around 5:30pm, Alexander had walked towards the village to meet Mary and escort her back to

North Bank Cottage. Presumably, this had been pre-arranged, or McLaren must have known approximately when to expect Mary. But why did McLaren feel the need to escort her? There was almost no crime ever recorded in the area, so her general safety could not have been an issue. We are not told if he escorted her through the village of Portencross on her way to West Kilbride. Could it have been that he wished to see her safely through Portencross for some reason?

McLaren met Mary about half way between Seamill and Portencross at the entrance to Ardneil Farm. They then returned together. Interestingly, McLaren made a point to mention that they met a stranger, a man, on the way back – they passed the time of day and moved on.

On arrival at North Bank Cottage, McLaren had milked the cow whilst the two ladies prepared the dinner. After they had eaten and tidied up, they had retired to the little sitting room where Alexander was to read to the ladies from a book by W.W. Jacobs. The book was entitled "At Sunwich Port" and was a fairly substantial humorous novel that had been written in 1902.

Again, I make note that the blinds were not drawn, despite it being a wet and windy night, and that Mary had positioned herself that she might easily see anyone advancing from

Portencross, if they were using a light.

The Interviews

As dawn broke on Sunday morning, many policemen from all over the area were ready and in place to conduct a thorough search of the area. A huge search ensued across the fields, along the path and to Fences Farm but no further tracks were found. Unfortunately, the rain through the night had washed much away. No further evidence was to be found.

There had already been some high-profile shootings that year that had made the press. The murderers in these cases had all been brought to justice, and the death penalty applied, which of course fed the public desire for gory details. Even by that first morning of the investigation, all parties were expecting a male perpetrator to be apprehended.

It was quite unusual at the time for the victim of an attempted murder to give several interviews to the press, particularly so for McLaren who was a typical Victorian character that valued his privacy – indeed, he came to live at North Bank Cottage for this very reason. Now he could be seen freely expressing opinions to the gentlemen of the fourth estate, knowing that those opinions would be spread far and wide as the gossip continued.

Did he think that his statements might help bring the culprit to a speedy justice? Or could he be trying to direct the investigation without actually naming the suspect? The latter may have been more in keeping with his character, if there was in fact a secret that he was hiding. Indeed, his words were to be a great influence on the investigation.

I also wonder if by giving these interviews McLaren was trying to send a message to his suspect, in the hope that they should surrender. If my suspicions are correct, which I will further explore in the proceeding chapters, then this would explain he was careful to ensure that the Glasgow Herald in particular had all the details it needed.

The Stranger

Naturally enough for a tourist town such as West Kilbride, the police frequently received reports of strange gentlemen wandering the village. One such report was of a man that had stopped at about three farmhouses looking for directions to Portencross. This may have been the same man that stopped McLaren and Mary Gunn in their walk home from the village of West Kilbride. The police visited many farmhouses to see if anyone had knowledge of the man returning from Portencross afterwards, but no sighting of him could be found after the time of the murder.

The public seized the sensational notion of a strange man lurking in the village, and many further sightings were reported.

A report of a suspicious man at West Kilbride station who jumped on a train without a ticket turned out to be simply a local businessman who had run out of money.

A single man that had stayed at a boarding house in the area was deemed to be enough out of the ordinary to investigate - to no avail.

Another search was started when a mysterious stranger was spotted in a plantation at Portencross. This turned out to be a poacher.

Some local golfers noted a black shape in the sea and feared that it might be the suicidal murderer. On investigation it turned out to be a perfectly normal sea creature.

Public suspicion was aroused when McLaren was found having an argument with a Glasgow University student on a local bus. But this was found to be of no value in the investigation.

Chasing the Leads

On the Monday following the murder, Chief

Constable Robertson-Glasgow arrived at the scene. Robertson-Glasgow had previously been in service with the Royal Irish Constabulary (the police force of the united island of Ireland pre-1922). There were some elements of this case that gave detectives the notion of an Irish connection.

Firstly, to shoot through a window in the dead of night was a peculiarly Irish method of assassination, albeit more usually connected with the political wars on that island. Secondly, the Webley revolver was the normal gun carried by serving policemen in Ireland. The public had been informed that the weapon was a heavy service revolver "of the Colt type", and indeed Colt guns did fire Webley ammunition, but the more usual gun of possession was the British Webley. Finally, there were several Irish farm labourers boarding and working in Portencross, who would need to be expertly questioned – such as Patrick Murphy (aged 40) who was boarding at Goldenberry Farm. None of these ideas were to bear any fruit.

Meantime, the police also explored the possibility that the killer was Mary Gunn's Canadian love interest who had come to Scotland to try and win back Mary's heart and, in failing, took more drastic measures. In contacting the Canadian police, it was found that the man in question had remained in Canada during the time of the murder.

An idea that the murderer had escaped by means of a boat to Millport was also discounted after all boats were accounted for. The police had also taken dogs to the area and searched all along the top of the cliffs and in and out of the long grasses.

Searches were made up the cliff face behind the cottage, where the long grass had to be cut back to see if any trace could be found of the murder weapon.

The notion of the boots caused considerable interest and one member of the public suggested that the suspect could have been a local golfer. In fact, the detailed report from the local newspaper was to give us a substantial clue in the solving of the murder. We shall consider this in further detail in Chapter 4.

There were rumours that the murderer might have committed suicide after the successful killing of Mary Gunn, but a search of the coastline produced no body.

Police resources were further tested by the suggestion that the weapon had been thrown into the sea – a very simple method of disposal. On the suggestion of a local pearl fisher, policemen

62

armed with glass-bottomed buckets undertook a large police search.

This is how the Glasgow Herald reported the matter on 27th October:

AYRSHIRE MURDER
DEVICE FOR SEARCHING THE SEA

The Ayrshire police have adopted a new device to aid them in their search for some trace of the assailant in the Portencross case.

To enable them to satisfy themselves that the sea opposite the cottage does not withhold from them a solution of the mystery they have ordered from a local joiner a set of boxes with glass bottoms, which will be used from small boats for the purpose of a search of the waters.

As has already been stated, the inquiries of the authorities were extended to Glasgow on Friday, and it was known that they had received information from a city source which was regarded as highly important. These inquiries were continued on Saturday without any material result. As it was understood that the police, since Friday at least, had been able to narrow

*down their investigations towards a more
definite objective, it may be taken that
their return to the view that possibly the
assailant committed suicide in the sea is
prompted by the non-success of the
inquiries in Glasgow.*

*The shore opposite Northbank Cottage, as
has been pointed out previously, consists
of a shelf of irregular rocks, which extends
along the coast for more than a mile.
From these rocks the tide never recedes
sufficiently to uncover the lower rocks and
shingle. Here and there, particularly off
the rocks opposite the cottage, there are
extensive pools of considerable depth.
Having satisfied themselves that it would
be fruitless to make further search for a
weapon or body among the brushwood
and rocks in the neighbourhood of the
house, the police have entered upon an
investigation of the sea at the point
indicated.*

*The boxes which are being employed are,
as stated, of wood, with glass bottoms and
with a handle on either side. The search is
conducted from over the stern of a rowing
boat. The searcher holds the box by the
handles, presses it about six or eight
inches into the sea for the purpose of*

avoiding the surface ripple, and gazes through the glass. Whether the searchers will be able to penetrate to the bottom remains to be tested, but it is not likely that the search will be hampered by the seaweed which clings to the thick profusion around the rocks. The operation can only be conducted when the sea is calm. It was intended to begin yesterday, but the conditions were not favourable. Should the sea be calm today the search will be entered upon.

Mr. MacLaren returned to Northbank Cottage on Saturday forenoon, after having resided overnight on Friday at a neighbour's farm at Portencross. The condition of his wife, who was removed to Kilmarnock Infirmary on Friday, is reported to be improving.

*During the week-end several rumours of arrests were current in West Kilbride, **Ardrossan**, and other towns in the district, but these were stated to have no foundation in fact.*

They had searched the rocks and seabed for any sign of the gun, but due to the long fronds of seaweed, once again the result was null.

Jessie's Recovery

On the Monday at North Bank Cottage itself, Dr More and a Dr Alexander conducted an autopsy on the body of Mary Gunn. All this time, the McLarens had remained at North Bank.

Above – a newspaper photograph of Jessie McLaren as she makes her way to the memorial service and send off of her murdered sister at the West Kilbride railway station on the Tuesday after the murder

The McLarens were members of the Barony Established Church of Scotland in the village. On Tuesday, a small service was held for Mary Gunn. Her body was placed in a coffin and loaded on to a train to be taken for burial at the Southern Necropolis in Glasgow, where both her

66

father and mother were buried. A small crowd gathered at the station to wish a final farewell, including the two McLarens. Jessie McLaren was still too weak to travel to Glasgow.

Later that day, Dr More examined Jessie's back and saw that the healing process was a little slower than he had hoped. It was therefore determined that she should be moved to Kilmarnock Infirmary where the nurses could attend her progress more effectively.

Above – Modern day Garnock Street in Dalry where Alexander and Jessie McLaren moved to after the murder.

For the period whilst his wife was in hospital, Alexander McLaren stayed sometimes with his friend Alexander Murray and his wife, at

Portencross Farm, and at other times he was able to return to the cottage. Despite renting North Bank Cottage until the end of 1914, the McLarens would never fully return. Jessie was finally fit to be moved at the end of 1913 and the two of them moved to a property owned by some old friends in Garnock Street, Dalry – the Hamilton sisters.

The Motive

In the early days of the investigation, the search for the killer was very broad. Both Alexander McLaren and his wife Jessie had stated publicly that they were unaware of any motive that could lead to such a crime. With the benefit of hindsight, we now know that the four main motives for murder can usually be reduced to Love, Lust, Lucre and Loathing - or any combination thereof.

The robbery (Lucre) motive was considered early in the investigation. Over the last few months, McLaren had been selling the livestock from his farm at auction. On the 16th October, two days before the murder, McLaren had attended an auction in Perth where he had sold some of the livestock from the farm for £100. He was paid by cheque, but it is possible that a potential robber may have mistaken this for cash. It was certainly rumoured locally that McLaren was wealthy.

However, no break-in had been attempted at the property, and even as McLaren had left the house for some 45 minutes after the shooting, Jessie attested that there had been no attempted entry. McLaren had only the sum of £15 in the house and about £20 in his pockets at the time but certainly no fortune.

With Mary Gunn's beauty in her youth, a consideration was of course paid to Love or Lust as a motive. The former Canadian boyfriend investigation had proved fruitless, but was there some other admirer that the McLaren's did not wish to disclose?

The fourth motive of loathing is harder to quantify unless we can find a reason why someone might be affected by this emotion. Alexander McLaren was well known in West Kilbride, as a member of the United Free Church and a subscriber to the library. He had already become known as a pleasant friendly person, and kind to know. On the face of it, one cannot imagine why another person might loathe him or indeed the murder victim, Mary Gunn.

In Chapter 4 below I shall expound a theory that the actual motive was indeed loathing.

We must remember that McLaren was an

evangelical and might not wish either his or Mary's name tarnished with any suggestion of tawdriness. Frustratingly perhaps for the McLarens, the investigation seemed to have stalled with no apparent suspect on the horizon.

Later in the week however - perhaps after the police read the report in the Ardrossan & Saltcoats Herald dated 25th October, 1913 which identified a hand made pair of boots worn by the murderer - the investigation moved quickly to Glasgow. I believe Alexander McLaren had now furnished the police with details of his suspicion, which never reached the public ear to protect the good name of Mary Gunn and the McLarens.

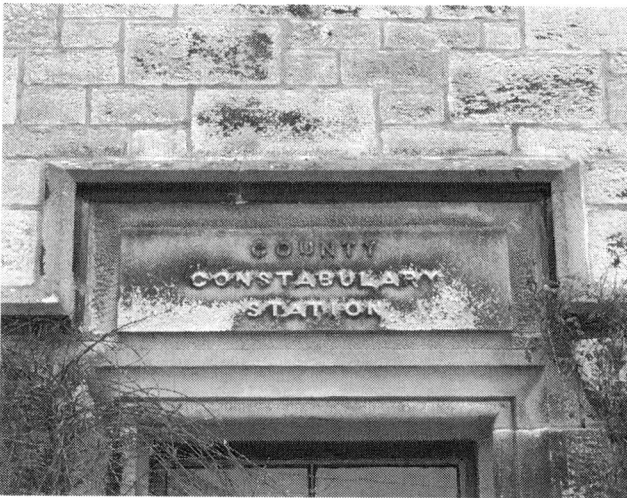

Above – The sign above the door of West Kilbride Police Station (now disused) as it appears today

An Arrest?

As the local papers went to press that week, the police made a bold announcement as though they were certain of the outcome. They stated that officers had been dispatched to Glasgow to interview a possible suspect and an "arrest was imminent". One can imagine that even the local police would not make such a bold statement, unless they were quite sure of a significant breakthrough.

Expectant crowds gathered outside the West Kilbride police station as the day wore on. An audible gasp could be heard when two men were ushered through the crowd and into custody, but these were simply two drunken rowdies who had been arrested locally.

Gradually the crowd dispersed as no exciting or promised developments occurred. The police never issued any further statement on this city investigation and it was gradually forgotten.

The week after the murder, the La Scala picture house in Saltcoats capitalised on the public interest in the murder by cancelling the ongoing run of Les Miserables. From the 31st October, they advertised a showing of a little-known Italian movie translated as "The Fatal Grotto". The movie was extremely popular, drawing large numbers.

By now the trail of the murderer had gone cold. No further evidence was to be found. No motive for the murder was ever discovered, and no satisfactory explanation for the mysterious murder has ever been advanced.

There was, however, a strange epilogue to the murderous tale. In late 1914, as McLaren had moved to Garnock Street, Dalry, Mrs Gibson of Shore House in Portencross launched a slander court action against him. The court action never came to trial, although it did provide us with evidence as to the identity of the Portencross murderer and, in my opinion, finally answer the question as to who killed Mary Gunn.

FRIDAY, OCTOBER 31, 1913,

LA SCALA
PICTURE HOUSE, SALTCOATS.

SPECIAL NOTICE.
LES MISERABLES will be discontinued after THURSDAY, 30th October.
FRIDAY and SATURDAY, 31st October and 1st November
ALL NEW PICTURES
WILL BE SHOWN, INCLUDING

THE FATAL GROTTO.

Above – The press notice changing the advertised programme one week after the murder

CHAPTER 4: Alexander McLaren

As we well know, the central character in this tale of murder is Alexander McLaren, brother-in-law of Mary Gunn. His interviews to the press were prolific in the days following the murder. The journalist Jack House, in his 1983 book "Murder Not Proven", even suggested that somehow McLaren might have been the murderer – the whole event being a botched attempt to remove his wife from a love triangle. Such a theory required his wife to be involved in this conspiracy or somehow suffer from selected amnesia where she had forgotten that her husband left the room just before the shooting happened.

Much of McLaren's life has already been detailed above, but we note that he was a serial entrepreneur that gradually built his capital with the help of his wife and her sister. This involved the three living together mainly in rural locations. The week after the murder McLaren described his relationship with the victim:

> *"She kept nothing from me," he said, "and treated me as a brother".*

Mary Gunn's last words *"Oh Alex, I'm shot"* would seem to indicate a closer than normal relationship. Though, it may have been a natural cry for help to the one person who could save her in such a tragic circumstance.

In the Victorian age, McLaren was regarded as the head of the household, and as such there would have been a reliance on his strength in times of trouble. My view is that McLaren had cultivated a home where he was the centre of attention of two adoring women.

Furthermore, as a small businessman he would have understood the importance of being in control, and from the outset would have sought to be at the centre of this entire investigation. McLaren was offended by the idea that any aspect of Mary's life could have been kept secret from him. There could be no suggestion of a murder theory without his direct involvement or even agreement. McLaren would have himself positioned at the centre of, and vital to, this entire enquiry.

McLaren was a short and stocky man. It could be argued that he was the ideal height to fire the shots through the lower left-hand pane of the window. The police certainly considered him as a suspect at the earliest opportunity – he was removed to the West Kilbride Police Station on the night of the murder, where he was also interviewed. His boots were compared to the prints found in the garden and his shotgun examined to determine if it could have fired the

74

bullets.

In the week following the murder, whilst his wife was seriously ill from the bullet wound she had received, McLaren gave many interviews to the press. He unduly influenced the direction of the investigation towards a particular man in Glasgow, who was thus interviewed and eliminated from the enquiry. As the newspaper sensation died, and his wife Jessie was taken to the hospital, McLaren found himself suddenly alone and devoid of attention.

Above – McLaren talks to an Ardrossan & Saltcoats Herald journalist the day after the murder – note his bandaged hand.

Gradually, during the months of November and December, he developed his own murder theory that he would tout to anyone who would listen – particularly in West Kilbride and Portencross. There was little evidence to suggest his theory was true, although the murderer may have been interviewed and managed to evade detection. Such were McLaren's cries for attention, a writ being issued against him for slander.

CHAPTER 5: Who Killed Mary Gunn?

When I first discovered the identity of the murderer, it occurred to me just how gender-blind the police had been during their investigation. McLaren (and also possibly his wife Jessie) had been directing the investigation along a particular suspect line. That line was ultimately found to be false but had given the true murderer enough time to cover her tracks.

There is no doubt that the murderer thought she had escaped the law. She was bold enough to commit this heinous crime, and hot-headed enough that in 1914 she launched a speculative court action to hurt Alexander McLaren once again.

The Portencross murderer was, in my humble opinion, none other than Mrs Elizabeth Gibson, proprietrix of the Shore Boarding House on the sea front in the tiny Portencross village, and almost the nearest neighbour to North Bank Cottage.

The Glasgow Herald reported on 4th December 1914:

> *"The pursuer avers that the defender falsely and calumniously made statements to the effect that she had participated in or*

had guilty knowledge of the murder of the defenders sister in law, MISS MARY GUNN at Portencross on October 18 last year. In consequence of the defenders statements an estrangement has resulted between herself and her husband, and her business has suffered very seriously.

"It is expected that application will be made for a jury trial."

The pursuer was Elizabeth Gibson and the defender none other than Alexander McLaren. Gibson had claimed that McLaren's false accusations of her involvement in the murder had damaged her personal relationships as well as her business. It should be noted that in Scotland, a slander action might be committed to a jury trial, such as the famous Tommy Sheridan case in recent years.

This charge was to be dropped suddenly with no explanation.

The Affair

Before we explore the motivation of Elizabeth Gibson, we must consider the aforementioned affair of May Gunn.

In the 1955 newspaper description of the crime,

journalist Jack House bemoaned the lack of motive for the murder. House had only based his investigations on the Glasgow Herald newspaper writings and as such must have missed this critical paragraph in the 25th October edition of the Ardrossan & Saltcoats Herald, that states:

> *"A story has been circulated to the effect that the late Miss Gunn had a love affair. Her sweetheart is said to be **very well off**. Questioned on this point, Mr McLaren said **he knew all about Miss Gunn's love affair**. "She kept nothing from me," he said, "and treated me as a brother".*

At first, I had assumed that the love affair being referred to was that of the Canadian adventure. Mary had started a relationship with a "young man" (as reported in many of the newspapers) in Saskatchewan. This relationship had not worked out, and Mary had returned to Scotland shortly thereafter. This man was investigated following the murder but was found to be still in Canada.

It is also interesting that the newspaper paragraph notes that the story had been circulated – presumably locally in West Kilbride, Seamill and Portencross. If people locally were chattering about such a relationship that McLaren himself had confirmed, it is likely that either the lovers had been spotted or that either Mary Gunn or

McLaren had been indiscrete and told someone of the affair.

The Edwardians were rather freer with their favours following the restrictive morality of the Victorian Age. The language used was different than that of the contemporary age, and as such it is possible that the "love affair" was not an extra marital relationship but simply a close romantic bond. However, due to this disparity we should not exclude the possibility of a true affair.

The fact that the affair was intended to be kept secret in the first place could lead to the assumption that the gentleman concerned was married or had some other reason for concealment.

In summary, the clues lead us to consider that we are looking for a married man who was conducting a relationship with Mary Gunn prior to her murder. It is possible that he was younger than Gunn and was "very well off".

Andrew Gibson

This exclusive information from the Ardrossan & Saltcoats Herald (when combined with the details of the 1914 slander trial) draws our attention to a new player: Andrew Gibson, husband of Elizabeth Gibson. In the period following the murder, the couple were to separate and ultimately divorce.

Andrew Gibson married Elizabeth Walker at 43 Windsor Terrace in Glasgow on the 2nd of August 1899, when she was just 19-years old and himself 29-years. They had both come from the same area of Glasgow and may well have grown up together.

I had wondered if Andrew had a military record prior to the wedding, which might have given him an opportunity to have a service revolver. Nonetheless, his marriage certificate states that in 1899 he was a journeyman shoemaker for his father's firm at 104 Renfield Street in the city centre.

The shoe making business was of the highest quality in the centre of Glasgow. Andrew's father was the Master shoemaker in the family firm whilst Andrew was the apprentice – known as a "Journeyman" in those days. By the time of the Portencross murder, Andrew too would probably have been a Master of the trade guild and would have held a responsible position. As now head of the firm and co-owning a respectable boarding house in Portencross, he would have been seen locally as "very well off".

Interestingly, his position would have given him

access to any number of gentlemen and ex-army personnel who most certainly would have known how and where to acquire a revolver.

The Gibson couple do not appear to have had any children. In 1912, Elizabeth rented the remote Shore Boarding House in Portencross from William Adams - the Laird of Auchenames. As her husband worked in Glasgow and often travelled all around Scotland in the commission of his work, I believe he could easily have purchased his wife a revolver for the purposes of protection in this rural environment and against potential attack in the boarding house.

In May of 1913, the McLarens arrived at North Bank Cottage where they quickly struck up a friendship with Andrew and Elizabeth Gibson. Alexander, Jessie and indeed Mary, like Andrew and Elizabeth, were entrepreneurs and so they would all have had at least that in common. Perhaps they spent time at each other's houses and consequently the dogs of the McLarens would be accustomed to the sound of Elizabeth's step, and her scent.

It is not hard to imagine that between May and October of 1913, Andrew Gibson could have formed a close relationship with Mary Gunn. He was now 43 years old, whilst Mary was 49. Of course, no one will know just how close this

82

friendship became, but I certainly believe it was friendly enough to cause considerable concern with Andrew's wife.

It is possible that by Saturday the 18th of October, Elizabeth Gibson had discovered Andrew's improper attentions towards Miss Mary Gunn. I suspect that Alexander McLaren had known of this discovery and was expecting some form of retribution.

Above – Shore Boarding House in 1913, shown here as the larger building in the middle of the three.

What form might that retribution take? An unseemly public confrontation was a good possibility – and so, I suggest, McLaren went to meet Mary on her way home from the village that day to protect her from humiliation. In the evening the blinds were not drawn as a form of guard, so that they could see if anyone was approaching the cottage.

In the 1914 slander action, McLaren accused Elizabeth Gibson of having "guilty knowledge of the murder". This passive statement shows that McLaren was never quite certain whether it was Elizabeth or Andrew Gibson that had committed the foul deed. From almost the outset, I believe that Alexander and Jessie McLaren thought the murderer to be Andrew Gibson and had thus directed the police. When this line of enquiry proved false, their suspicion then alighted upon his wife Elizabeth.

There is some physical, though mainly circumstantial evidence, from the newspaper reports that point directly at Elizabeth Gibson as the Portencross murderer that killed Mary Gunn. Is there now, one hundred and five years later, any evidence to suggest that Elizabeth Gibson was hot-headed or rash, where she might take some form of drastic action? With the benefit of hindsight, we can analyse the court action in 1914 where she drew attention to herself by means of a slander trial.

The Slander Trial

If we can presume for a moment that Elizabeth

was innocent of the murder of Mary Gunn, it would seem perfectly reasonable that her lawyer would have advised against raising a slander court action, potentially with a jury. These were the days of the death penalty for murder and with nobody currently under suspicion surely this kind of slander action was unwise to say the least. Who could foresee what new information might be produced in a court of law that could be persuasive of her guilt? Perhaps there was a dark-side to Elizabeth, eager to start litigation even against these risks.

Almost as soon as the action was raised it was dropped again, and we may never know why. Nor do we know why her husband Andrew abandoned his wife and moved back to Glasgow. Both of these facts are rather suggestive of some underlying issue that never made the public domain.

If we can recall, about a week after the murder, the police sensationally turned their attention to Glasgow where they expected to make an arrest. This would have been presumably when they went to interview Andrew Gibson at the suggestion of Alexander McLaren.

Why did Alexander McLaren believe that Andrew Gibson had committed the murder? Had they been engaged in an argument? Did McLaren know that Elizabeth had discovered the extra marital affair? Either of these scenarios may be possible, but I would advance a third option. I have suggested that McLaren enjoyed being at the centre of attention, that he was egocentric in character. The first three bullets were fired at him – the primary target. Therefore, it is not unlikely that McLaren believed that whoever had shot that night had intended to eliminate him, and that the other shots were wayward attempts again at eliminating him.

McLaren would therefore have considered in the earliest stages of the murder investigation, in his egocentric way, who might want to eliminate him. He knew that Mary Gunn doted on him, and so perhaps it was a case of jealousy. Or perhaps McLaren had indicated to Mary that he disapproved of her affair, and so Gibson had seen McLaren as an obstacle.

Any of these ideas pointed towards Gibson as a suspect. McLaren therefore directed the police towards his residence in Glasgow. If Andrew Gibson had not had an alibi for that night, he could have quite possibly been hanged for the murder of Mary Gunn.

CHAPTER 6: The Day of the Murder

Let us now reconsider the day of the murder and how, armed with our new suspicion of the murderess, it may all have happened.

We have eliminated all events in the day as not relevant to the case, until around 5:30pm. We recall McLaren went to meet Mary Gunn as she returned from her shopping trip, meeting her about the road to Ardneil Farm (halfway to Seamill). He escorted Mary back through the village of Portencross and, most importantly, past Shore Boarding House - the residence and business place of Elizabeth Gibson. I have suggested that this may have been to protect Mary from a public scene.

Elizabeth Gibson could have watched them pass the house, infuriated by Mary's guardianship. Perhaps she viewed McLaren to be protecting Mary Gunn as if she was an innocent party. She would have waited, boiling in anger, for darkness to fall. She had three hours to wait until it would be dark enough for her purpose, and during that time she would have thought carefully about how to approach the cottage, with what weapon, and how she would make her escape.

In the evening around 8:30pm, as the three victims sat down by the fireside, we recall how the blinds were curiously left open so that an unencumbered view of the approach to cottage could be had. This allowed the McLarens to keep watch for a torchlight down the path from the little village, which might herald the arrival of Elizabeth Gibson to create a scene.

It would be highly unlikely that Alexander McLaren would have expected, before the murder, that Andrew Gibson would take arms against him to a violent conclusion. Such action was out of character, but it was more certainly an extremely rare occurrence in Scotland. The later police investigation would show that Andrew Gibson was in Glasgow that evening. If he had been discovered to be having an extra marital affair, he may not have wished to be near his inquisitive or angry wife on that particular night.

Perhaps earlier in the day, or the day before, McLaren had argued with Andrew Gibson. He had suggested that Gibson stop seeing Mary Gunn until his existing marital status was resolved – or simply to stop seeing Mary altogether. In which case, McLaren may have considered the possibility that Andrew Gibson would arrive to argue further.

Elizabeth Gibson, seething still from her discovery, waited until it 8.30pm when it was dark, drew the loaded revolver that her husband had given her, and approached the tiny cottage by stealth that they should not see her approach. The McLarens' dogs would sense nothing out of the ordinary as they were used to Elizabeth Gibson, and perhaps she even stopped to reassure them.

She wore her new, flat-soled, Halstead boots. Her husband was a quality shoemaker with his own family business in Glasgow and I would suggest that these boots were made especially for her moving to Portencross in 1912. So good were these boots that they were likely rarely worn, and consequently the three-basket logo that was to appear in the plaster cast impression during the investigation was clearly recognisable.

On the night of the murder, as soon as the boot impressions were found, the police compared them to the boots worn by Alexander McLaren – they did not fit. Regrettably we are not told if McLaren's boots were smaller or larger than the impressions. We are told that McLaren was a short and stocky man, but we do not know what shoe size either he or Elizabeth Gibson might have had.

Nonetheless, in my view, the boot prints are an excellent indicator as to the identity of the murderer.
I have earlier suggested that the police seemed gender blind, possibly due to the suggestion by

McLaren that the murderer was male (where he and Jessie had suspected Andrew Gibson). This misdirection lead the police to interview Andrew at length in Glasgow, but importantly gave time for the real murderer to cover her tracks.

Above – A newspaper photograph showing McLaren inspecting the boot prints left in his garden by the murderer, overseen by the police. Once again we see McLaren in the thick of the investigation and potentially steering or directing it. This is how McLaren was able to release the information concerning the "Holsted" boot prints with handmade logo to the Ardrossan & Saltcoats Herald – a clue that was subsequently missed for 105 years.

In Chapter 1 above, I mentioned how in the 1950s the Glasgow journalist Jack House had painted a picture of Portencross as a lonely, beautiful, remote spot. However, in 1913 it was a relatively bustling agricultural and tourist town with many residents and a lot of visitors. A glance at the 1911 census shows that there were many agricultural labourers and whole families cramped into single room bothies.

The area was not as dark as Jack House had suggested in the 1955 literature, either. The full moon fell on October 15th and should have lasted until October 18th, the night of the murder. At the very least it would have been gibbous waning. An approach by stealth on North Bank Cottage would not have been easy. Although, the two cottages to the north of Shore Boarding House were empty on the night of the murder - an advantage for an unobserved approach and escape.

So, I suggest, Elizabeth waited until it was reasonably dark and looked out of her window to ensure that the coast was clear. She slipped out of Shore House onto the farm path and made her way in the moonlight night until she reached North Bank Cottage. Her pathway was clear. Perhaps if she had met anyone on her way she would have stopped the commission of the murder, but as there was no body to implicate her, she carried on.

Elizabeth approached the tiny cottage closely
along the side of the wall, taking great care not to
be seen by the occupants of the sitting room. She
had observed them in the room as she approached
and would have clearly seen that the blinds were
not pulled down. We are told in the newspapers
that as the taxi containing the police later
approached the cottage, the golden square of light
from the window was clearly visible from several
hundred yards away.

She aimed her revolver at McLaren, the primary
defence of Mary Gunn. She fired a shot that
shattered the little windowpane of glass tore off
the tip of McLarens' left index finger, forcing its
way through his book.

The newspapers of the day sensationally claimed
that the bullet had passed through the book. "At
Sunwich Port" by W.W. Jacobs is a relatively

substantial novel of around 350 pages, and so if it were closed then such an action would have been rather difficult. We must therefore assume confirmation of McLaren's statement that the book was open. McLaren made various statements regarding the book. In one, he says that he had just begun reading, which suggests that one side of the book would have been thinner, and in another statement he says he had read four chapters. Either way, if the bullet did pass through the book it would have been on the left-hand side of it.

The shock made McLaren jump up. Quickly, Elizabeth fired two more shots in succession but by now McLaren was behind his armchair. He shouted "Floor! Floor!" to the two ladies in the room to instruct them also to take cover.

On hearing this instruction, Elizabeth turned the revolver to target Mary Gunn. That next shot went wide of the mark and hit Jessie McLaren non-fatally. Elizabeth fired the final two shots – the first to strike Mary Gunn and the second to drive through her heart, killing her. Mary slumped to the floor uttering her final words "Oh Alex, I am shot!".

Above – North Bank Cottage with the farm track in the foreground as it was in 1913

Even after all of this, Elizabeth thought to shoot some more, perhaps to finally eliminate McLaren. With only the sitting room light to guide her, she opened the revolver to reload. She had never been given instruction that the spent bullet casings needed to be removed from the barrel of a revolver (possibly indicating that the gun was never expected to be used), and as she fumbled with the revolving barrel it fell to the ground. This was later found by the police. I maintain my position that the shooter was no professional marksman.

The cordite burns on the whitewash wall indicate how near she was to the side of the cottage, and therefore how fearfully she had tried to hide her identity. A more confident shooter would not have adopted this angle. She had approached at this angle, and remained there during the whole event, so that she would not be recognised.

In a panic, she retreated into the darkness, running quickly up the farm track to reach Shore Boarding House within a few minutes.

By this time, we know that McLaren had run out of the house and was frantically searching the grounds surrounding the little cottage. With no sign of the assassin he released his two dogs. In my humble opinion, McLaren had expected to charge out of the cottage to discover Andrew Gibson, to easily overpower him, and bring him to justice. Perhaps this erroneous belief dictated his next actions as he ran up the farm track and entered the side gateway to Auchenames Estate.

After William Adams had raised the hue and cry, McLaren ran along the outer footpath to get additional support from his farmer friend, Alexander Murray. This path carefully avoided the outside of Shore Boarding House. Together, they returned to William Adam's house to be informed the police were on the way.

Above – North Bank Cottage with the farm track in the foreground as it was in 1913. The gap in the rocks is known locally as "the throughlet" and the pathway leads to the small clachan of Portencross to the south.

McLaren and the farmer started walking west towards the farm path. Just as they reached the outside of Shore Boarding House, a taxi drew up with two policemen and the local practitioner Dr More aboard. Perhaps, at that very moment it had been the intention of McLaren to confront the Gibsons, but with the arrival of the police he decided to allow the officials to take over. Elizabeth Gibson by now had probably concealed the murder weapon, which would never again be seen.

A 21st Century Investigation

When I first realised that Elizabeth Gibson was

the Portencross murderer, I could not understand the gender blindness of the police investigation. As detailed in the previous chapters, it dawned on me that the McLarens had directed the police investigation towards Andrew Gibson - a suspect of theirs from the outset. It was not until later that McLaren might begin to suspect Gibson's wife, Elizabeth. It was this mistaken misdirection that was to afford Elizabeth Gibson the time to cover her tracks. The evidence was concealed, and any punishment escaped.

Initially, the McLarens had tried to implicate Andrew without suggesting any impropriety that might tarnish the reputation of Mary Gunn. Perhaps with noble intention, they tried to protect the Gunn name from any sense of scandal. Similarly, they had reason to ensure their own name was not dragged in such an unseemly way through the tawdry press. Understanding such motivations in the Edwardian era gives vital context to an otherwise unsolvable case.

In all the press reports I have read, the reporters are directed towards a male suspect. The public, with a sense of determination, and possibly through dread that this might be the start of a terrible serial, were frantic to discover the perpetrator. The Edwardians responded by reporting any and all strange goings on by men far and wide. As we have seen, all manner of strange theories emerged regarding the commission of the murder, the motive and the ultimate escape of the perpetrator.

The police investigated over the next few days, fully in the public eye, and with large amounts of resources being deployed at the investigation including huge numbers of men from all throughout the County.

As the days wore on, Elizabeth Gibson would have had ample opportunity to finally dispose of the weapon. Perhaps this was thrown out to sea as suggested by a member of the public, buried in the garden of the Shore Boarding House, or perhaps she took it with her when she finally left the business behind. I feel sure that the delay in the police investigation whilst they followed false leads must have also given her an opportunity to discuss the murder with her husband who would surely have had his suspicions.

Of course, had Andrew Gibson taken those suspicions to the police, the high-end shoe business that he and his father had built up in the city centre of Glasgow would have been ruined. There was therefore a clear incentive for the continued silence of the Gibsons.

Above – Modern day photograph of the premises in Glasgow where Andrew Gibson conducted his business.

On November 11th, the Chief Constable of Ayr issued a reward notice offering £100 for information that would lead to the arrest of the perpetrator. The only person who might have been able to offer such information with evidence was Andrew Gibson himself. He was unlikely to implicate his wife, as his own name would have been ruined and his business in Glasgow would have ended after many years.

When the police investigation stalled, and they had still not alighted upon Andrew Gibson as a prime suspect, it is my own opinion that McLaren finally accused him as having a likely motive, although the newspapers report that a source in the city gave the police their break. At last the police thought they had the breakthrough they needed to solve and apprehend the murderer.

Even as officers were speeding to Glasgow to interview Andrew Gibson, local police were making a sensational statement to the press that an arrest was imminent. Crowds gathered outside the West Kilbride police station expectantly waiting to see the miscreant. We should remember that West Kilbride was a tourist town, and even though these events were in October, the scandal would have drawn additional sensation-seeking tourists and journalists.

The crowds outside West Kilbride police station were to go unrewarded for their curiosity and the police issued no further explanation.

Without the police file, we shall never know exactly what then happened with the investigation. My interpretation of events would be that Andrew Gibson had a watertight alibi for the evening of the murder, and consequently the police looked rather foolish to have made the statement that an arrest was imminent. Nor are we to know just how watertight his alibi was, as the police file has been subsequently lost. Was he with family members that were able to testify to his whereabouts? Or was he away on his journeyman business? Certainly, there was enough time given inadvertently (by McLaren and the police) to allow Andrew and his wife to create their cover.

So, the police investigation gradually got cooler. The world went back to business as normal. The McLarens left North Bank Cottage and moved to Garnock Street in Dalry. Two spinster sisters they had met whilst Alexander had managed the ironware store owned the Garnock Street house, and there was plenty of room for Alexander and Jessie to remain as long as they wished. Jessie McLaren never returned to the site of the murder of her younger sister.

I believe that sometime in late 1913 or early 1914, Alexander must have come to the incredible realisation that the murderer was potentially Elizabeth Gibson and not her husband Andrew. Perhaps it was then that he started spreading the rumour that she had been involved - but he certainly had little or no evidence beyond the circumstantial, and the knowledge that he alone kept secret. Perhaps he ultimately did tell the police of his suspicions, but with almost no evidence to enforce his theory, they may have declined to act.

CHAPTER 7: The Final Act

So, there the mystery has stood for 105 years.

Following the post-mortem examination of her corpse in her own home by Dr More and a Dr Alexander, Mary Gunn was buried very quickly in the Southern Necropolis of Glasgow. I have visited the Southern Necropolis several times and have not yet found her grave. There are over 250,000 people buried in the Necropolis and the surviving gravestones are in a very deteriorating condition.

Sometime not long after the slander case was dropped in 1914, Alexander and Jessie McLaren moved away to Canongate in Edinburgh. I believe this may have been part of the deal to settle the case. Sadly, Alexander was to die there in 1916 aged 64. Jessie McLaren lived until she was 85 years old and died in Edinburgh in 1936.

Elizabeth Gibson gave up the boarding house at Portencross and went to live in Stevenston in North Ayrshire. She was divorced from Andrew Gibson and again took her maiden name, Walker. She died in 1954.

There the case would have died - unsolved and unremarked upon - were it not for the famous Glasgow journalist, Jack House. Some 42 years after the murder, House wrote a weeklong series of daily articles for the Glasgow Evening News. The research material he used to structure his articles came from the original articles published by the Glasgow Herald in the aftermath of the murder. In those pre-internet or microfiche days he did not review the other newspapers' much more detailed writings on the case.

Even in 1955, the mysterious unsolved murder caused a public stir. The thought of an unknown assailant firing a gun through a sitting room window and escaping, never to be found, horrified members of the public. Murder was a most topical subject earlier in that year as the public debate was raging as to whether or not the notorious murderess Ruth Ellis should be to publicly hanged. I do not think that Jack House had any idea at that point that there were clear parallels between the ultimate fate of Ruth Ellis and what might have been with the guilty party of the Portencross Murder. By now, following two world wars, people perhaps placed a higher value on human life – Ruth was the last woman hanged in this manner.

It is somewhat sad that the murderer died just one year before Jack House the Glasgow journalist was to write his series of articles for the Evening News.

As another generation passed, in 1984 Jack House was asked to present and write a TV series on famous Scottish murders where the case remained unsolved or the perpetrator had escaped the clutches of the law by means of the curiously Scottish verdict of a jury - "Not Proven". It was perhaps because of the remote Scottish scenery, or that North Bank Cottage remains now almost as it was all those years ago, that the particular episode on the Portencross Murder once again sparked public interest.

And here we are, yet another generation has passed, and interest is yet again thrown on the curious and mysterious case of the Portencross murder. It is a terrible shame that the police have lost the file with their investigation notes, but it is remarkable the amount of detail that can be gleaned from the thorough work of local journalists writing at the time. Even so, it is to be hoped that the golden age of investigative journalism is yet to come.

In the end, why was nobody ever caught and charged with this murder? Certainly, there was plenty of call on police resources. The trail of the murderer had never been hot enough to go cold. No clues were ever found that gave sufficient evidence for an arrest or even a proper police interrogation – save for Andrew Gibson, perhaps. Enough time had gone by for Elizabeth Gibson to hide the evidence forever. Then, the push towards the First World War caught everyone's attention.

During the war, the Police were of course thinned as more and more men were sent to fight, whilst those left at home were charged with maintaining the peace during wartime.

On the page following a description of the peace celebrations held in London on Saturday 19 July 1919, a 'special correspondent' of the Daily Herald wrote of an 'epidemic of violence and atrocious murder' sweeping the country:

> *"Human life has never reached such a low valuation as today ... It can be traced to the atmosphere of blood and violence necessary for the perpetration of a war of the kind we have just survived. This atmosphere, carefully created by an intense propaganda campaign, has gradually altered the moral aspect of the country at large, and has sown such seeds of perversion and lust for violence that the crop will be heavy and bitter".*

There would be no incentive to cast about looking for the murderer of such a crime as Portencross.

The one person who might have gained energy

anew to make accusation of the murderer, Alexander McLaren, never did. Both he and his wife Jessie set sail on the SS Letitia on the 28th June 1929 bound for Quebec in Canada where Alexander's brother awaited them. In 1929, they were 76 years of age. A gravestone in Quebec states that Alexander died on 13th May 1939 at the age of 86.

The murderess herself died in Stevenston in 1954, one year before Jack House wrote his celebrated articles. Perhaps if his articles had upset her she might have confessed, although the death penalty was still in force in these years.

Neither the McLarens nor Gibsons had any children. No future generation was to discover the awful truth.

The murder weapon was never found, likely having been thrown out to sea opposite Shore House, off the pier or buried in the garden.

On Wednesday October 16th 2013, two days before the hundredth anniversary of the murder, the Ardrossan & Saltcoats Herald ran an article asking if the murder had happened today if it would it have been easier to solve. The newspaper interviewed Inspector Brian Skimming from Police Scotland's North Ayrshire Community Policing Team to get a modern take on the crime. He reflected that the latest statistics for solving murders are 98.4% and so he had every confidence that modern techniques would have solved the crime.

As if the murder were not strange enough, another quirk in the case appeared in the "True Crime" magazine dated November 2013. A writer, Alex F. Young revisited the case and declared that in the 1980's he had interviewed a police officer involved with the original case. That policeman declared that the murder weapon had been found concealed in a rabbit hole a few month's after the murder. Another claim was that a gun had been found to be missing from the armoury at Glasgow University and as there had been a witness report of McLaren arguing with a student on the Portencross charabanc bus, there was a possibility of the murderer being a student.

There are a number of problems with this account. Firstly, I am personally aware that the murder weapon was never found as police interviewed my father and grandmother when a revolver was found in Portencross – it was subsequently identified as a WW2 gun. From what we know of Alexander McLaren, we can be virtually certain that had a weapon been found, he would have immediately announced it to the press. McLaren enjoyed being the centre of attention, and was keen to keep the case in the public attention at least until late 1914.

The notion of a gun being hidden in a rabbit hole in Portencross was a rumour being spread around West Kilbride in the days after the murder. It was not true and denied by the police consistently well into the 1970's. Perhaps the policeman or Mr Young had got a memory confused after such a long time.

Secondly, the student theory was indeed investigated by the police and found to be a red herring. McLaren himself could provide no clue as to this lead – no motive could be discovered. In the heady days of 1913, revolvers were not hard to acquire – the article in True Crime is written from a late 20th Century perspective where gun licensing had become the norm. In Glasgow, in the early 20th Century, shootings were not uncommon – even hunting was a relatively common past time as we have seen.

Another problem with the student theory is the method of the murder. Why would such a student need to hide their identity in their approach to the property and during the shooting? Also, the dogs did not query the approach of the stranger.

Mr Young said was able to identify three possible students who might have had access to a missing revolver – even in the 1980's. It is therefore hard to believe that even with the extensive manpower resources deployed by the police on the murder investigation, they were unable to trace the exact individual concerned and find whether or not they were guilty of the heinous crime.

The Officers Training Corps (OTC) at the University of Glasgow had been established in 1910. Modern History Professor Dudley Medley (fondly nicknamed "Deadly Mudley") could foresee the oncoming turpitude and had successfully approached the University for permission to build a drill training hall, mess canteen and armoury on University Avenue. These additional facilities were completed by 1913, ready for use when the students returned in October. By the date of the murder, students had been on campus for less than two weeks. It seems unlikely that in that time, one student member of the OTC could have gained access to the armoury, stolen a weapon unnoticed, planned and committed the crime whilst also evading detection and apprehension. Even were it to be so, it would surely be a relatively short list of all those students who could have had access to the armoury at such an early stage of it's development and the police might easily have therefore apprehended the murderer.

If indeed a student had taken the revolver, why would they not have returned it to its home in order not to alert suspicion?

The establishment of the OTC and the arming of students had not gone unnoticed with the public in Glasgow. Concern was expressed from many quarters, and certainly it was in the forefront of attention in some quarters. Even so, I did search for any report of such a missing weapon at the University armoury and could find none. It is my view that the rumours of a missing weapon and a student criminal were purely Edwardian sensationalism – as indeed was the rumour of the finding of the weapon concealed down a rabbit hole.

I am therefore forced to consider the sensational claims in True Crime magazine as probably false.

There was of course a Glasgow connection to the case in the person of Andrew Gibson. One can only speculate if the supposed argument on the Charabanc was not between a student and Alexander McLaren, but with Andrew Gibson. Although this would indeed be convenient to my own theory as to the murderer, it would still seem obvious that any such argument having taken place would have given McLaren the necessary clue as to the actual perpetrator. The only reason I could come up with as to why McLaren might not have wanted to immediately put forward the name of Gibson as the murderer, would be so that he did not embroil the poor dead Mary Gunn (or indeed himself) in any kind of scandal. Instead, he started by directing the investigation towards a male by recording his views in the newspapers. Finally as the investigation seemed to be cooling, McLaren pointed the police directly at Andrew Gibson and the investigation switched to Glasgow. Expecting an immediate arrest and even after announcing it to the waiting public, the police were to discover that Gibson had an alibi for the night in question.

This also answers another question – why in particular did the murder take place on a Saturday night when the area was most likely to be busiest? My own suspicion is that Elizabeth Gibson felt very alone when her husband was in Glasgow and she was left in Portencross. Her knowledge of the love affair between Mary Gunn and her husband would have been festering inside her until it all became too much. The sight, in the afternoon, of Alexander McLaren walking by with Mary Gunn as if he were protecting her, was perhaps all too much, and as the anger boiled insider her, the evil plan to injure at least two of them was born.

I am not convinced that murder was the full intent of Elizabeth Gibson – otherwise I doubt she would have taken such care in the approach to the cottage with stealth. I believe she probably intended to frighten or injure the occupants of the little cottage as a matter of some revenge, then make good her escape – but the sudden movement of the people in the room whilst she was wildly firing the bullets, had the fatal consequences we know today.

So, I rest my case dear reader. The murderer was not a male, but a female – Elizabeth Gibson. A little gender blindness by the police and the newspapers and considerable misdirection by Alexander McLaren allowed Mrs Gibson to cover the evidence and thereby make good her escape.

In the photograph below we see McLaren examining the covered boot prints in the garden. McLaren involved himself in every aspect of the investigation and thereby was able to steer it. In other photographs shown earlier, we see how he conducted prolific interviews with the newspapers – closely watched by the detectives. His announcement to the Ardrossan & Saltcoats Herald that the boot prints had a hand-makers mark directed the investigation straight to the door of Andrew Gibson, quality Glasgow shoemaker and husband of Elizabeth Gibson – the owner of the Shore Cottage Boarding House at Portencross. McLaren also identified the boots as "Holsted" as the newspaper printed – being actually "Halstead" or a precursor to the ankle length Chelsea boot worn by both men and women. The gender blindness of all concerned assumed a male murderer, until such time as Elizabeth Gibson was able to hide the murder weapon and probably even the boots. We know the boots were a small size such as might be worn by a woman – during the early stages of the investigation they were compared to the boots worn by Alexander McLaren himself, and found to be even smaller than his boot size. McLaren was himself a relatively small man for the age, and his boot size was small even for the day.

The publicity surrounding the boots gave rise to a great deal of speculation. Some suggested a crazed golfer that would have worn boots, and we have seen how a student was considered who would have perhaps had a smaller size shoe.

There is no doubt that McLaren was the central character of this investigation. Even Jack House in the 1950's would sense this – giving rise to the possible notion that the wounded victim could have in fact been the murderer himself. This notion had arisen from a misinterpretation of a newspaper statement by McLaren regarding Mary Gunn's on going love affair (I believe with Andrew Gibson).

Within the year, McLaren would come to the realisation as to who the guilty party was, and accuse her in public, resulting in an initial rather rash court action – an action quickly dropped lest she be exposed.

We cannot convict Elizabeth Gibson, nor even come to know what actually caused the events of this frightful night – she, and all other parties, are now long since dead. We can only speculate. Perhaps now the case can be regarded as solved and Mary Gunn can finally rest in peace.

CHAPTER 8: Conclusion

In the foregoing tale of murder and deception I have weaved in and out of different aspects of the story and introduced many characters. I therefore thought to summarise my own conclusions of the murder in order that anyone might easily revisit the case or any part thereof - especially if the police file should ever return to light.

Murderer

> The villain was Elizabeth Gibson, owner of the Shore Boarding House.

> Evidence included the Halstead boots, newly made and to a standard that her husband was very capable of manufacturing, the fumbled bullet at the window scene of the crime, the close proximity of her home, the recognition of the dogs, and the likelihood of her owning a service weapon for protection due to the nature of her business. Additional evidence included the statement by McLaren that he knew of Miss Gunn's love affair, coupled with his 1914 accusation, the police interview of her husband, Elizabeth McLaren's proclivity toward rash action as in the case of the 1914 court trial, and the other evidence per

below.

Weapon

A Webley (or possibly a Colt) Mark III or IV service revolver given to her by her husband for protection.

Evidence was fairly conclusive - the bullet that was removed from the heart of Mary Gunn, following her death, and examined by ballistic experts, was found to be calibre of around 0.45 (Webley and Colt both 0.455) as used in a revolver of the Colt type.

Opportunity

Elizabeth Gibson lived at Shore Boarding House, less than half a mile from the scene of the murder. The opportunity presented itself when darkness had fallen, and the three individuals had retired to a sitting room, failing to pull the blinds down and conceal their exact location in the room.

Evidence from the statements of both Alexander and Jessie McLaren gave full details of the opportunity as it was presented to any murderer.

Motive

The motive for the murder was jealousy or loathing. Andrew Gibson, who was slightly older than Elizabeth and younger than Mary Gunn, had become close or attached to the latter – McLaren was aware of this by his own statement a week after the murder. Elizabeth, Andrew's wife, had discovered this. On the Saturday of the murder she had been stopped from confronting Mary Gunn, by the protecting presence of Alexander McLaren.

Evidence includes the October 1913 statement by McLaren that he was aware of the love affair, the 1914 statement of McLaren in which he accuses Elizabeth Gibson, and the police suspicion and interview of Andrew Gibson. The subsequent divorce of Elizabeth and Andrew Gibson very quickly after the murder is an important clue. The boarding house quickly ceased to trade after the murder, the reason for which was given by Elizabeth herself where she blamed it on the accusations of McLaren regarding her involvement in the murder.

Escape

The murderess escaped by quickly returning to her home, thus evading detection by McLaren and his dogs. An early failure by McLaren to name the possible criminal allowed the opportunity for Elizabeth to conceal the murder weapon and her boots.

The evidence for this is that, despite extensive searches on the night of the murder, the dogs, McLaren and the police were unable to find any clue of the route of escape of the murderer. Even the following day no tracks were to be found. The murder weapon, boots, and motive were never discovered or revealed.

Cover-Up

Following the murder, why did the name of the criminal not become known? There were only four people who could possibly have known the true identity of the murderer -

Elizabeth Gibson would have faced the death penalty had she confessed, she may well have been interviewed by police but without a confession and hard physical evidence (the police did not connect the boot prints with her husband because they were looking for a male murderer and discounted them in this instance), there was no possibility of a conviction.

Andrew Gibson failed to accuse his wife, since to do so would potentially ruin his business in Glasgow and her business in Portencross (although he tellingly did not become involved in the 1914 slander action, and carefully distanced himself from it).

Alexander McLaren suspected Andrew Gibson of the murder, he had little actual evidence beyond what he knew about the relationship between this married man and his dead sister-in-law (October 1913 statement to the Ardrossan & Saltcoats Herald). He was therefore unable or unwilling to make a direct named accusation in the press, but he did make a reference to the love affair in 1913 and he also accused Elizabeth Gibson in public leading to the 1914 slander action. Alexander may have taken the matter further had he not died in 1916 less than two years after the slander action.

Jessie McLaren had even less information or evidence than her husband and probably did not want to see her sister's name muddied in the press. She was in thrall to her husband and did not make any statements. Once she had recovered, and had been removed to Edinburgh, then subsequently suffered the loss of her husband in 1916, she perhaps had no desire or will to pursue the guilty party.

Although the police did reopen the case several times, no further significant evidence came to light that would convict the murderess. The police may well have had their suspicions as to the identity of the killer, but without any significant evidence the murder was to remain unsolved for these 105 years.

Character

One thought has crossed my mind since writing the first version of this book. Alexander McLaren revelled in attention – he seemed to be the centre of the lives of this little family of three. When Mary had been shot, she did not call out the name of her sister, but of her brother-in-law. Earlier in the day, Alexander had gone to meet Mary coming back from the village and they had walked and talked together.

Even when Mary had emigrated to Canada, she did not settle and had returned to be with Alexander and Jessie. These are suggestive of a very co-dependent relationship. It is hard to determine how much Alexander had cultivated the closeness of this relationship.

I never subscribed to the theory that Alexander had some part in the murder, but nor did I find his reactions afterward as wholly normal. The police allowed him to play a full part in the investigation and report to the press – he portrayed a charming, charismatic personality. He clearly revelled in the attention given by the press (further back in his life he had built a Gospel Hall so that he could speak to assembled crowds – again seeking attention). When the press attention waned, he again found attention when the court action was raised and dropped. He had been going around the village talking to anyone that would listen, to the detriment of Elizabeth's business.

The question has entered my mind - could Alexander McLaren have been displaying mild sociopathic tendencies?

Then there was Elizabeth Gibson. She was known for her snap temper. There is the evidence of the sudden court case, and its sudden withdrawal. If she was indeed the murderer, could we be considering the possibility of psychopathic tendencies?

Could it have been that there was a duel between a sociopath and a psychopath? I am no psychiatrist, but it is an interesting notion for thought.

Therefore, I present my case to the court of popular opinion and hope that perhaps we are at least one step further in solving the mystery of who killed Mary Gunn.

Appendix 1 - Portincross?

In many of the newspaper reports the spelling of Portencross is Portincross. I thought my readers might like to understand a little of the rich history of the area along with the reason why there are two common spellings.

The older spelling of the tiny clachan or village is Portincross or Portincors. This relates to a period around 1606 when Patrick Crawford, the 12th Laird of Auchenames, married a distant relative – Jean Craufurd of Crosbie. The marital assets then formed a massive stretch of agricultural land from the edge of the Hunterston Estate, along the coastline and inland to Crosbie (medieval Corsby) at the North East of West Kilbride. The name Portincross therefore simply refers to the Port in the Crosbie estate. The tiny village established by, and fully owned by the Laird of the Auchenames Estate until the 20th Century.

The farm pathway to the north of the peninsula and the road inland to Seamill and West Kilbride mentioned in the present case has a much older tradition. The Innse Gael (foreign Gaels or Irish Norse) formed this path when they landed in the 10th Century. We evidence this by the incredible find of the 9th or 10th Century Hunterston Brooch from along the edge of the road. On old maps this road was called the "Haef Weg" which is Norse

Scaldic meaning "the way to the sea" and is now used by villages in the name of Halfway Street.

Some time in the mid 14th Century, Robert II built a small fort at the port, and in the 15th Century the Boyd family demolished that one and built the castle we see today as a watchtower over the Firth of the Clyde.

So for the period after the beginning of the 17th Century, the name Portincross was used for the old post by the castle and the tiny village all round it.

During this period there was no gap in the cliff face that we now know as the throughlet (see the picture in Chapter 4). This meant that the piece of land that North Bank Cottage now stands on, was surrounded on three sides – two by cliffs and one by sea. It made a perfect grazing ground for mainly sheep. Consequently it was named "Pencross" or "Pencors" – meaning the sheep pen of the Crosbie estate.

So Portincross and Pencross were two distinct places, albeit with the primitive map-making throughout the 17th, 18th and 19th centuries, and as traditional livestock farming waned, the two names often labelled against each other.

As the tourist economy grew in the little area, a

tiny post office was established in the village of Portincross around the very beginning of the 20th Century, it was decided to label the entire seaboard, including North Bank Cottage, a mixture of the two names and so Portincross became Portencross for the purposes of mail delivery and thereafter became known so.

Other Books by Stephen Brown

ISBN 9781909805323
The Portencross Armada Conspiracy

In which the author finally identifies the only Spanish Armada ship to land in Scotland in August of 1588, and the subsequent cover up.

ISBN 9781909805019
A History of the West Kilbride Town Crest

In which the author explores the interesting history of how a village town crest was developed purely for the tourist industry.

Both available worldwide and posted at the local rate to each county by Amazon

Further information can be obtained from The Transparent Publishing Company

sales@transparentpublishing.co.uk

About the Author

Stephen Brown is a gentleman of no particular consequence or merit. He originally trained as an accountant and has served many companies in a senior capacity throughout his career. He is a serial entrepreneur having sold one of his businesses and now runs another.

His passion is for the history and heritage of the area where he grew up – West Kilbride. His father grew up in Portencross. In 2015, he established and now runs the "Being West Kilbride" Facebook Group that has about 2,400 members. He has written several books on various subjects relating to his local history.

He is married, lives in West Kilbride, and has four children.

Printed in Great Britain
by Amazon